FROM **HELLO** TO **GOODBYE**

Proactive Tips for Maintaining Positive Employee Relations

FROM **HELLO** TO **GOODBYE**

Proactive Tips for Maintaining Positive Employee Relations

Christine V. Walters, MAS, J.D., SPHR

Society for Human Resource Management
Alexandria, Virginia
www.shrm.org

Strategic Human Resource Management India
Mumbai, India
www.shrmindia.org

Society for Human Resource Management
Haidian District Beijing, China
www.shrm.org/cn

The Society for Human Resource Management (SHRM) is the world's largest association devoted to human resource management. Representing more than 250,000 members in over 140 countries, the Society serves the needs of HR professionals and advances the interests of the HR profession. Founded in 1948, SHRM has more than 575 affiliated chapters within the United States and subsidiary offices in China and India. Visit SHRM Online at www.shrm.org.

Cover Design: Shirley E.M. Raybuck
Interior Design: Shirley E.M. Raybuck

Library of Congress Cataloging-in-Publication Data

Walters, Christine V., 1961-
From hello to goodbye: proactive tips for maintaining positive employee relations / Christine V. Walters.
    p. cm.
Includes bibliographical references and index.
ISBN 978-1-58644-206-4
1. Personnel management. 2. Performance standards. 3. Problem employees. 4. Employees--Dismissal of. I. Title.
HF5549.W337 2011
658.3--dc22
                        2010037438
                                                            10-0499

Contents

Backword vii

Chapter 1. When All Else Fails:
Terminating the Employment Relationship 1

Chapter 2. Document, Document, Document! 19

Chapter 3. Coaching, Counseling, and Correcting. 39

Chapter 4. Employee, Where Art Thou?
Managing Disability and Leave Issues 57

Chapter 5. Maintaining an Inclusive Workplace. 75

Chapter 6. What's in a Name? Properly Classifying Your Workers 85

Chapter 7. Employee Handbooks: Read 'Em and Weep? 101

Chapter 8. Welcome Onboard. 115

Foreword. Practice Your Passion! 123

Appendix A. Pre-Termination Checklist 127

Endnotes 129

Index 137

Acknowledgements 141

About the Author 143

Additional SHRM-Published Books 145

Backword

You've seen it happen time and time again, right? We work backwards. That is, we begin focusing on an employment relationship as it nears its end; e.g., when our employee is not performing as expected and we are thinking about letting him go. That's when your legal counsel or HR administrator asks the eternal question, "Do you have any documentation?" Then when you let the employee go you receive a charge from the U.S. Equal Employment Opportunity Commission (EEOC), your state, or local commission.

It is in that spirit that this book is written — to reflect not how this process should work but how it often happens: backwards. You may start at the end of the book, which is the beginning of the employment relationship; or start at the beginning of the book, which is the end of the employment relationship. Either way, when you finish this book, you will have some new insights, practical tips, and ideas for ensuring that the door does not hit you on the employee's way out.

There are just five things to consider as you read this book:

1. Those of you who know me know that my favorite answer for many questions is two words, "It depends." No strategy, practice, or procedure will work well in every situation or for every person. So keep in mind that this book is intended only to serve as a guide to offer tips for proactive practices, not the right answer for any particular situation.

2. For the reasons cited above and more, this book does not constitute the rendering of legal advice. You should contact your company's legal counsel for guidance on any particular employee situation.

3. The use of the pronoun he/him/his is gender neutral and applies to either gender or both.

4. We often hear about "best" practices. As you read this book, you will find that I refer to "proactive" practices. Because businesses vary so much in what, where, when, and how they do business, I find there are few "best" practices. I find there are, however, myriad proactive practices — and that is the focus of this book.

5. Make the most of this book. Each chapter closes with practical tips. Consider these as you review and update your company's policies, practices, and procedures. There are also myriad links and resources provided in the endnotes for you. It is my hope that this book can become a resource that you can use repeatedly.

1

When All Else Fails: Terminating the Employment Relationship

Well, here you are at the end of the employment relationship. You have coached, counseled, and attempted to correct, yet the employee's behavior is still not meeting expectations. Thus, you have concluded that it is time to terminate the employment relationship. So what are some final steps you should take to ensure you have dotted and crossed your proverbial i's and t's? Consider the following.

Pre-Termination Checklist

Use the following five questions as a pre-termination checklist. This can help in a variety of ways — from preparing your presentation for an unemployment insurance hearing to defending your action before a federal or state agency or local human relations commission, and, perhaps more importantly, helping to ensure consistent treatment of all employees who are in similar situations.

Forewarning

Are you able to describe when and how you set your standard or expectation for this particular employee? Or is this a case where your position is, "Aw, come on, everyone knows you are supposed to ..." or "Everyone knows you are not supposed to ..." While this might hold true for lying, cheating, and stealing (although certain actions of select political, business, and other leaders might lead one to conclude that *nothing* can be

1

taken for granted), it is not the case for most performance standards. Take, for example, excessive absenteeism or tardiness. I find this is a common standard that managers believe with all honesty and conviction that everyone shares and thus there is no need to define it. But, when discussing the matter with peers and colleagues, they regularly find that their expectations may not match those of their peers, including managers and supervisors in the same department, as well as across the organization. Try the following exercise with your management team, particularly those managers working in the same department. Ask them to write down on a sheet of paper their answer to the question, "How many unscheduled absences in a six-month period do you consider to be excessive?" Then go around the room and have them answer one at a time while you record the answers. You can be pretty much guaranteed that you will find differences, sometimes vast, among their answers. Now there may be very valid reasons for having different standards in different departments. For example, if I am an HR administrator in a hospital (which I was for nearly 10 years), it is likely that my attendance and punctuality standard for my HR staff would be different and possibly more lenient than the standard a director might have in a nursing unit for the direct care providers. Why? There is a valid business reason: The impact to business operations when my HR staff is late is less or at least potentially less than when a direct care provider is late or absent. So remember that what you take for granted as a reasonable expectation may not be shared by others; communicate your expectations from the beginning of the employment relationship. How? Consider developing a new employee orientation checklist list (see chapter 7). When an employee does not meet your expectation, provide objective and specific examples of desired performance (see chapter 3). And, throughout these processes, remember to document these activities (see chapter 2), because only then will you be well positioned if and when the time comes to demonstrate how and when you provided the employee with forewarning of your expectation.

What if you find managers within the same department have different expectations? Talk about the differences and why they exist.

Are the rationales justified based on business need or are they subjective? For example, let's say there are three managers in the accounting department: one in accounts receivable (A/R), one in accounts payable (A/P), and one in payroll. Each supervises one to three employees. One manager believes an employee should have no more than six unscheduled absences in a six-month period; the second manager believes an employee should have no more than four unscheduled absences in a six-month period; and the third manager believes an employee should have no more than two unscheduled absences in a six-month period. The managers should focus on the impact that employee absences have on business operations, compare and contrast the impact, and understand why they have set different standards. The A/R manager may indicate that unscheduled absences have the potential to delay the collection of money from clients and customers, which reduces the company's cash-on-hand, which might impact its bond rating or leave less money available for investments and thereby reduce interest income. The A/P manager may indicate that unscheduled absences have the potential to delay payments to vendors, which may result in late fees or charges, causing unnecessary costs to the company. The payroll manager may indicate that unscheduled absences have the potential to delay the processing of payroll, which could result in fines if employees are not paid in a timely fashion, not to mention the bad employee morale that may be created. All three concerns are tied to business operations and are valid. They might not, however, justify such a broad difference in the expectation. Thus, the managers might work with human resources to determine what the company's average absence rate is and agree upon one standard that all three managers will use for the entire accounting department.[1]

Evidence

Do you have evidence to corroborate your position that the employee has failed to meet expectations? Evidence usually comes in one of three forms.

Employee's admission. Often an employee will admit to having done something incorrectly or inappropriately. But don't stop there. "Why" can be a powerful inquiry; just knowing what an employee did may not be enough. Understanding why the employee did or failed to do something often opens doors to learning about systems, processes, training, communication, or other systems that need some fine tuning or are just not working. If that is the case, both you and the employee now have the opportunity to learn. You might establish a new training program or implement a new (or adjust an existing) policy or procedure. Sometimes, however, the employee does not admit to an error or omission despite evidence to the contrary. Thus, you will need to consider what other evidence you have to substantiate your claim.

Witnesses. You may have one or more witnesses who will report that they saw or heard or otherwise have knowledge of the alleged behavior. Having two or more witnesses is generally better than having just one witness. But what if you have just one witness and it becomes a matter of one employee's word against the other? Consider whether the witness would have any reasonable motive for fabricating the report. Does the employee have any reasonable motive for denying the allegation? This is where judgment comes into play. While it is subjective, you will need to determine whether it is more likely than not that the witness is telling the truth. Sometimes you may be left with a non-finding; that is, you cannot determine whether it is more likely that one employee is telling the truth over the other. In this instance, you might take this as an opportunity to meet with the employee to coach, counsel, educate, and/or reinforce a policy or expectation with regard to conduct or work performance. Document that meeting (see chapter 2); if the matter should arise again in the future, your documentation may help establish the likelihood that the employee has, in fact, engaged in the alleged conduct or failed to perform as expected or required. The same could also be the case of multiple witnesses who may, on occasion, collude to create a story to get a coworker they dislike in trouble. Be open to considering these options. Often you have to conduct a credibility assessment. You may have to determine which story is more accurate. This is where seeking assistance from human resources or another management colleague can help. An objective set of eyes and ears may help you decipher the truth of the matter. If you don't have any witness(es) or the employee's own admission, don't give up yet. Try and find some tangible evidence.

Tangible evidence. You may have tangible evidence — such as time-clock punches, video recordings from security cameras, e-mail or voice mail messages, Internet logs, written notes, etc. — that will corroborate your allegation. If you have none of the above, you may want to re-evaluate your impression or opinion of the employee's performance and ensure that you are not biased in any way. This does not mean you had any ill-intent; rather, sometimes we can be influenced by what we have heard about an employee's performance, attitude, conduct, etc. If you hear that an employee is initiating gossip about a coworker and there is suddenly a report of a rumor being spread around your department about a coworker, you might immediately assume that you know who started the rumor or gossip. Don't assume; get evidence to substantiate your position.

Proper Investigation

Have you conducted a proper investigation prior to making your final decision to terminate employment? Just because you have your evidence as listed above doesn't mean the case is closed. Perhaps one of the most important elements of conducting a proper investigation includes getting the employee's side of the story. It has happened more than once that an employee tells the story of being called into the manager's office and asked to give his side of the story regarding an incident and, after he does so, the manager then turns over a sheet of paper that was sitting on the manager's desk during the entire meeting. The sheet of paper turns out to be a written notice of corrective action, which the manager then issues to the employee. What message did the employee just receive? That action speaks volumes to the fact that it did not matter what the employee said; the manager had already made up his mind. Be open to explanations, even if the conduct is unacceptable. Take sleeping on duty as an example. I remember a situation in which a director came to human resources and wanted an employee fired for sleeping on duty. The employee had already received written, corrective action for sleeping on duty, and this was also in a direct patient care area so the potential impact in failing to respond to a patient could have had serious negative consequences. The director had done a good preliminary job of gathering evidence. The director produced statements from at least two coworkers who had observed the employee sleeping. When I suggested the director get the employee's side of the story, however, the director declined. The director's position was that there was no acceptable reason for sleeping on duty, and since the employee had already been warned once, termination was warranted. So, the employee was fired for sleeping on duty. The matter went through the grievance process and then to arbitration. The arbitrator reinstated the employee without back pay. Why? He wrote that while he had reason to doubt the employee's veracity (she said she was not sleeping, only resting her eyes) he added that by the director's own admission she had failed to conduct a thorough investigation; she had failed to get the employee's side of the story before terminating the employee. What could be a reasonable excuse for sleeping on duty? Perhaps the employee had just been prescribed a new medication for a medical condition and the medication made her sleepy. Without getting that information first, you might have not only terminated the employee without knowing all the facts, you may also have a discrimination charge on your hands for failure to provide reasonable accommodation under the Americans with Disabilities Act.

Lack of Discrimination

This element goes beyond what you may think when you hear the term "discrimination." It goes beyond legally protected classes such as age, race, religion, national origin, disability, gender, etc. It goes to the issue of equitable treatment. Ask yourself, "Is it your obligation as the employer to treat your employees equally or equitably?" Most likely the answer is the latter. You may not want to treat all your employees exactly the same or equally; you want to reward your top performers and provide incentives to those who go above and beyond. Likewise, you may not want to impose the same sanctions or penalties to employees who are not similarly situated or who have different situations. Take attendance and punctuality as a common example. A key question is whether you have treated this employee the same as others who have been similarly situated. This is where we distinguish between equal treatment and equitable treatment. Let's say you are preparing to terminate an employee who has been coached, counseled, and received corrective action for excessive absenteeism, and who has now incurred a total of 10 separate and unscheduled occurrences in the last six months. So you might ask, has any other employee incurred 10 unscheduled occurrences in a six-month period and *not* been terminated? If your answer is "Yes" then your next step is to determine why you are treating two employees differently who appear to be similarly situated. Perhaps it is because they are not, in fact similarly situated. While both have incurred the same number of occurrences in the same period of time, the circumstances may not be the same. Imagine the first employee's absences were all related to the same reason, such as caring for a critically or terminally ill relative, and the employee has worked for you for several years and has an otherwise exemplary work record. The second employee's absences, however, have been for a variety of unrelated reasons, none of which are particularly unique or exigent, and this employee has worked for you for less than one year and is only a marginal performer. While the two appear on their face to be the same, the circumstances are quite different. In this case, issuing corrective action to the latter employee and not the former may be justified.

Penalty Meets the Offense

Finally, ask if termination is warranted; e.g., is it reasonable to expect that any lesser penalty would correct the behavior? If the employee has already been coached, counseled, and received corrective action on three prior occasions, then it may be unreasonable to expect that a fourth would make any difference. But when an employee has not been given at least one or perhaps two opportunities to correct the behavior, it might be reasonable to think that you could salvage the relationship, not to mention getting a positive return on your investment (ROI) on the time and money you have invested in the recruitment, selection, hiring, and training of this employee.

Policy Versus Practice

Managers may ask, "But, if employment is at-will, why do I have to jump through all these hoops? Why do I have to coach, counsel, and correct if employment can be terminated at the will of either party?" (see chapter 6). The key is in considering what you must do as compared to what you should do, for any variety of reasons. And even that is difficult, since what "should" be done is often assessed in the eye of the beholder; e.g., what is best for the employer or the employee. Barring the existence of any employment contract or collective bargaining agreement to the contrary, you do not have to coach, counsel, or correct prior to termination unless you are in a state that does not recognize at-will employment, such as Montana.[2] But go back to the beginning of this chapter and you will find the answer. You help to protect yourself and your company and reap the greatest ROI on your recruitment dollars when you protect your employees. Whether you have a corrective action policy or not, and even if you have a very clear and express at-will employment policy in your employee handbook, also consider your past practice. It is likely you have given other employees opportunities to correct their behavior or performance informally, even if not formally. So, ensure your action is consistent with not just your written policy but also your past practice. Do so not because you have to do the same thing for every employee but because you need to be able to distinguish why you did "x" in one instance and "y" in another.

Here is another common situation I have encountered. An employer has a leave of absence policy that reads that an employee may take an unpaid leave of absence not to exceed 30 days. On the 31st day of leave a manager wants to terminate an employee's employment. The HR representative, however, is aware of at least two prior instances in which "good" employees had *not* been terminated immediately after 30 days. This does not mean the manager cannot go ahead and terminate employment. It should, however, raise a flag to simply ask, "Why?" How is the current situation different from the previous situations? Is there a good business justification for treating this employee differently? For example, perhaps the two prior incidents involved long-term, high-performing employees who needed only two additional weeks of leave and it would have taken at least that long to fill their positions. The current employee may have worked for the company less than one year, has documented poor performance, and the employee's expected return to work date is "unknown."

Remember that your company's practice can be just as important as your company's policy. Also, read through your employee handbook or employment policies. Run a "search" for the words "will result" or "will receive," and where it refers to corrective action or termination, consider replacing it with "may result" or "may receive." Don't back yourself into a corner. If you indicate that something "will" happen, you may lose the ability to exercise management discretion, and you may lose the ability to treat employees equitably versus equally. When you indicate that something "will" happen, then you must take the defensive position of justifying why you did *not* do something. When you indicate that something "may" happen, you retain the right to determine if and when it will happen.

Adverse Impact Analysis

Do you know the demographics of your last 10 involuntary terminations, or your discharges in the last six months? In the last year? If not, you should. It is a proactive practice to track and monitor the age, race, and gender of your terminations. Employers with 100 or more employees (and certain federal contractors) are already required to collect data on the gender and race of their employees for EEO-1 and affirmative action purposes. Employers with less than 100 employees and those not required to have written affirmative action plans should consult with legal counsel about collecting this data, inviting employees to self-identify using a voluntary self-identification form. Once collected, you can conduct a wide variety of analyses, such as the age, gender, or race of employees who are involuntarily terminated (as well as who voluntarily terminate) as compared to the same demographics of your workforce at large. For example, if 20 percent of your total workforce is age 40 or above (the ages protected against discrimination under the Age Discrimination in Employment Act or ADEA) yet 50 percent of your involuntary terminations have been employees age 40 or above, those figures may appear to be statistically, significantly disparate. This may lead you to analyze those results and try to determine why a significantly larger percentage of your terminations are employees age 40 and above than are represented in your workforce as a whole. The same analyses may be conducted based on gender and race. Also consider whether a statistically significant number of terminations are occurring in a particular department or under a particular manager or business unit. Here you may see a pattern that may not necessarily give rise to a legal issue but rather to an opportunity to dialogue with that manager about his management style, expectations, and sharing the objective data so that manager can consider why separations from his department are occurring at a rate higher than the company average. Being forewarned is being forearmed. You want to be aware of these trends before they are pointed out to you by an external party such as the federal Equal Employment Opportunity Commission (EEOC), state or local human relations commission, or a plaintiff's attorney.

Also, consider if there have been any unusual recent events such as a female employee informing you that she is or is trying to become pregnant; an employee requesting leave under the Family and Medical Leave Act; an employee filing a workers' compensation claim; or an employee engaging in any other legally protected activity. If the answer is "Yes," this does not mean you should not proceed as planned. It will, however, enable you to review and confirm your pre-termination checklist (see Appendix A).

Finally, tracking the demographics of your voluntary terminations can be valuable as well. It may be proactive to understand not just why employees are leaving your organization (addressed in exit interviews below) but who is leaving. Are there any groups that voluntarily leave your organization at a statistically significantly higher rate than other groups such as men, women, minorities, people under age 40 or 40 or above? Exit interviews can be a great way to learn more about why people are voluntarily leaving your organization and what practices you might enhance to increase retention. See chapter 8 for more information about stay interviews and retention strategies.

Exit Interviews

Exit interviews can be a great, easy, and inexpensive way to gather data, proactively monitor the reasons your employees are leaving, and look for trends. I find most employers who conduct exit interviews do so for employees voluntarily leaving and not for employees who are involunarily terminated. But when asked what they do with the data the answer is, "Nothing." The data is collected but not used in any practical way. Exit interviews can be conducted in person or electronically. Using an Excel™ spreadsheet, you can track the results by department, location, job classification, race, gender, age, and more. This data can be very valuable to not only signal any adverse trends — such as a statistically significant separation rate for men versus women, for persons age 40 and above, or for minorities — but to also provide feedback to department directors and plant managers who may have a higher than average turnover rate as compared to the organization as a whole.

Consider the following:

- Do you know what your company's current turnover rate is?

- Do you know what your average cost per hire is?

- Do you know how those rates compare to the standard rate for your industry?

- Are you tracking separations by departments or locations to watch for trends that indicate separation rates that are higher than the company average as a whole?

- Do you know why your employees are leaving? Are the separations predominantly voluntary or involuntary?

- What are the key reasons employees are voluntarily separating? Is it for better wages, and/or benefits?

These are just a few metrics of which you may want to be aware, whether you are the HR administrator for your company or a business owner, manager, or supervisor. There are a number of resources for finding formulas and tools by which to calculate and track these metrics.[3]

Why conduct exit interviews? There is the business case. Every time an employee leaves it costs your company money: from advertising, to interviewing, to conducting reference and background checks, to bringing the employee on board, and providing training and education on your company's policies, procedures, and job expectations. All these add to the learning curve during which your new employee's productivity may reasonably be below expectations as they are oriented and learn your way of doing things. So, if you can retain your top performers, you can save the company money. And, if the company saves money, that leaves funds available to enhance benefits, compensation, and more.

Why else should an employer conduct exit interviews? Have you ever been surprised to look at your mail and see the return address from the EEOC or your state or local commission on human relations? Why would an employee file a charge of discrimination with a government agency without ever bringing the concern to the employer's attention first? The answer is "trust." Trust is a big issue for employees. Sometimes it is a matter of believing that the company or a management representative will retaliate in some way against the employee if he complains internally. Sometimes it is a matter of believing that the employer will do nothing to rectify the situation. I find the latter even more frequently than the former. The person or practice that is frustrating the employee has gone on for a long period of time and is well known to the company, at least to several members of management, but nothing has been done to correct the matter. Often it focuses on a management team member who lacks certain interpersonal skills or is perceived as being a bully. With no trust or confidence that the company will do anything about it, the employee seeks an external resource.

Ensure that your company has a policy that provides one or more resources to whom an employee can report any work-related concerns, particularly those related to wage discrepancies, discrimination, or harassment. Also ensure that it is your company's practice to promptly investigate such concerns and take immediate and appropriate remedial action.

Severance

When it comes to involuntary separation from employment, the question is sometimes asked, "Should I offer this employee a severance package?" This practice is common in the case of an individual job abolishment, individual or group layoffs, or plant closings. A severance package is sometimes offered when a long-term employee is separated through no fault of the employee but it is determined that the individual is no longer a "good match" for the job. It is wise to have legal counsel draft or review any severance package you offer, particularly if you include in the agreement a waiver of the employee's right to sue your company. Most severance agreements include such a waiver. The agreement often offers the employee salary continuation or severance pay for a certain period of time (and sometimes continued benefits such as health care coverage) in exchange for the employee waiving his right to sue the company for a wide variety of possible claims under federal, state, and local laws, as well as common law.

Another question often asked is, "If I give one person a severance package, am I obligated to do the same for every other employee I terminate?" As described earlier, this is a question of equal versus equitable treatment. An employer should consider why it is offering this benefit to one employee and not another. There can be myriad reasons that may justify this difference in treatment, such as length of service and the reason for termination.

For persons age 40 and above, the Older Workers Benefit Protection Act (OWBPA) requires that, in order for such a waiver to be valid, the agreement must include the following elements:

1. It must be written in a manner calculated to be understood by the individual, or by the average individual eligible to participate in the

severance program. Employers should take into account such factors as the level of comprehension and education of typical participants. Consideration of these factors usually will require the limitation or elimination of technical jargon and of long, complex sentences.

2. The entire waiver agreement must be in writing.

3. The waiver agreement must not have the effect of misleading, misinforming, or failing to inform participants and affected individuals. Any advantages or disadvantages described shall be presented without either exaggerating the benefits or minimizing the limitations.

4. The waiver agreement must refer to the Age Discrimination in Employment Act (ADEA) by name in connection with the waiver.

5. The agreement must advise the employee in writing to consult an attorney before accepting the agreement.

6. The waiver must not require the individual to waive rights or claims that may arise after the date the waiver is executed. This does not prohibit the enforcement of agreements to perform future employment-related actions such as the employee's agreement to retire or otherwise terminate employment at a future date, so long as such agreement is not contrary to any other requirements of the ADEA.

7. The waiver must be in exchange for consideration in addition to anything of value to which the individual already is entitled. This means the employer must provide the employee with something, such as severance pay, that is in addition to that to which the individual is already entitled in the absence of a waiver. For example, if your company has a policy in its handbook that provides that any employee whose job is abolished will be provided with two weeks' pay, then the employer must provide the employee with more than two weeks' pay in order for the waiver to be enforceable.

8. A waiver agreement must give an employee a period of at least 21 days within which to consider the agreement. An employee may

sign the waiver before the 21 days has expired but must be given at least 21 days. If an employee volunteers to sign the agreement the same day he receives it, it may be a proactive practice to advise the employee to take some additional time, read the agreement thoroughly, and to consult with an attorney before signing the agreement.

9. The agreement must also provide the individual with a period of at least seven days following the execution of such agreement (the day the individual signs it), to revoke the agreement. The agreement shall not become effective or enforceable until the revocation period has expired. Thus, it can also be a proactive practice to wait to issue the first severance payment until at least the eighth day after an employee has signed the agreement.[4]

In the case of a group termination or exit incentive program, the same rules as described above apply to waivers in severance agreements for persons age 40 and above except that the employer must provide up to 45 days to consider the agreement. The employer must also provide each employee with additional information including but not limited to eligibility factors; time limits; job titles and ages of all employees who are eligible; and the ages of all individuals in the same job classifications or organizational unit who are not eligible.[5] This is why it is advisable to have an attorney review these agreements, whether for one individual or for a group of individuals, to ensure that your company is complying with a number of federal, state or local laws and regulations that dictate what these agreement must have (or not have) to be enforceable.

Unemployment Insurance

Another common question of employers and employees is, "Will this employee be eligible for unemployment insurance?" That answer rests with the state agency reviewing the claim. Each state has its own code for granting, denying, and administering benefits paid from the state's unemployment insurance (UI) trust fund. A good answer to give an employee may be to advise him to go ahead and file and let the employee know that the employer does not make that final determination but the state will determine eligibility. Although the rules vary from state to state, there are some commonalities. Generally, an employee may be eligible for UI benefits whether the employee quits or whether the employee is fired. The question in either case is "Why?" If the employee quit for reasons connected to the job, such as a change in wages, hours, or some condition of employment, then the employee may be eligible for benefits. An employee might also be eligible if he quit for a reason not connected to the job but for a compelling personal reason, such as to care for a terminally ill family member. In this instance, the employee may be required to show that he sought an alternative, such as a flexible schedule or transfer to another position, before resigning. If the employee is fired for some level of misconduct, then the employee may be disqualified depending upon the nature of the misconduct, the employer's policies, and whether the employee received any advance notice (i.e., coaching, counseling, or corrective action) prior to the termination. Once again, you can probably see that documentation can be critical to successfully defending why an employee should or should not be eligible for benefits (see chapter 2).

Employers pay a tax for UI benefits that, for most employers (non-profit employers may be taxed differently), is based, in part, on the company's experience rating. The more claims that are paid to your employees, the higher your experience rating and the higher your UI tax premium may be. Documenting performance problems and talking to your employee about the need to improve, as well as setting goals and objectives, can save your company money.

If you have never been to an unemployment insurance hearing, call your HR administrator or the person who handles the company's UI claims and ask if you may attend the next hearing for one of your employees who has left the company. The experience can be quite educational and can give you insight into how your state's agency assesses separations, what documentation they are seeking, and how you can save your company money.

Practical Tips

- Get the big picture. Even if you are sure termination is the correct next step, run it by your HR representative or legal counsel. While your plan of action may be consistent with the past practice in your department, human resources can monitor and provide you with the overall company practice to ensure consistency across the organization, watch for company-wide trends or patterns, and ensure that any termination is well-documented and based upon valid business reasons.

- Don't just open your employee handbook to be sure termination is in accordance with your policy; be sure it is also consistent with how the company has treated other employees in similar situations. If it is not, then you should have a bona fide and business-related reason for treating this employee differently.

- Conduct an adverse impact analysis to be sure this termination will not appear to establish a pattern or practice of treating members of any protected class (women, minorities, persons age 40 or above) differently from other legally protected groups. If it does, be able to provide a bona fide business reason as to how and why you have arrived at your decision.

- Follow your pre-termination checklist.

2

Document, Document, Document!

How many times have you asked a manager or been asked by human resources or legal counsel for documentation when it comes to issuing corrective action or terminating an employee? Is it better to have none, or some? Well, that depends upon the quality of your documentation. If your forms, notes, and performance appraisals are not accurate, then they can become weapons that a plaintiff's attorney can use against you. Too often it is the case when a manager wants to terminate an employee for unsatisfactory work performance that the most recent performance appraisal indicates the employee's performance meets or even exceeds expectations. Why? Sometimes it may seem easier to soft sell a performance appraisal and avoid the conflict of setting expectations and quantifying what aspects of performance are unsatisfactory. Other times it just seems like a hassle to find the time to sit down and document an employee's unsatisfactory work performance. What you document, and where and how you document, can vary, but doing so can be critical to supporting your business justification for taking adverse employment action; e.g., firing, not promoting, or issuing corrective action to an employee. Without good documentation, it may be hard to show that your reasons were business related and not based upon the employee's membership in a protected class. Here are a few tips.

What

Hopefully you are in your particular job because you have a passion or at least a preference for what you do. Whether you own or manage an auto body shop, lawn care service, or property management firm, or are in the academic, health care/human services, or any other business or industry, it is hopefully because you have a particular interest in that line of work. What you likely did not anticipate (except for those of you reading this who are HR professionals) is managing all the myriad issues that come with managing employment relationships.

The good news is that you are not expected to document every conversation that you have with every employee. You should document by exception. Document the exceptionally good and the exceptional not-so-good events, activities, and behaviors. If you go to work tomorrow and everything pretty much goes as expected, you would likely document very little or nothing with regard to employment activities. If you go to work tomorrow, however, and overhear an employee make a rude or derogatory comment, you might document that. In this case, it need not be formal, perhaps just a note to the file (not the HR file but to a "working file" you might maintain on your employees) or in your calendar of events. And don't forget the positive. When we talk about documenting performance it seems it is so often focusing on ensuring we have back-up for an upcoming, unsatisfactory performance appraisal, decision to not promote, termination, or other adverse employment action. Give the same dedication and attention to excellent performance. When you receive a customer or client compliment, then jot a note, make a copy, or put a special notation in the employee's file and share it with the employee. We can all use a pat on the back every now and then.

Where

Documentation does not have to be formal. As described above, it can be a casual note that is placed in a manager's "working" file that is kept in the manager's desk and not in the employee's HR or personnel file. On the other hand, documents such as corrective or disciplinary action notices, performance appraisals, or letters of commendation are usually placed in the employee file. These become a part of the regular employment record and the employee may have access to these records, in accordance with your state law and/or company policy. Some states require that an employee be permitted access to these records at certain times and under certain circumstances. Check with your legal counsel, because how you maintain and use certain documents can determine whether they can be "discovered" in anticipation of litigation.

When

I find a common question is, "When do I move from documenting in my 'working' or informal file to issuing corrective action that will go into the employee's HR or personnel file?" Documentation should be a constant and regular practice. When you move from this type of informal documentation to the formal notice of corrective action may be dependent upon many factors, including the severity of the behavior, frequency, prior coaching or counseling, the employee's intent, and more. For example, if an employee intentionally punches a coworker, you may take formal corrective action immediately (following a proper investigation, of course). On the other hand, if an employee is late one morning, you may be more likely to mention it to the employee but wait until a second, third, or fourth lateness in a particular period of time before issuing any formal corrective action. If two employees make the same procedural error, you might also decide to issue corrective action to one and not the other because you have already coached the former on the procedure on one or two prior occasions and this is the latter employee's first procedural error. Each instance should be assessed on a case-by-case basis to determine the most appropriate action.

The performance appraisal is an area that frequently lacks consistency. Many companies have a policy that reads that performance appraisals (or evaluations or reviews) will be conducted annually. Be sure that is defined. Does that mean the appraisal will be conducted on or about the same date every year for all employees, such as January 1? Or does that mean appraisals will be conducted on each employee's anniversary date determined by the employee's date of hire? You may set any date you like. Once that date is set, however, be sure the appraisals are completed in a timely fashion, particularly if your policy reads that they "will" happen rather than the "generally will" or "may" happen annually. Delaying or skipping appraisals may give the appearance of adverse treatment if one employee has not had an evaluation in the last two years while others have regularly received annual performance appraisals. Or imagine you want to issue corrective action or terminate employment of the employee described above because his performance is now unsatisfactory. If the employee was not given an appraisal and feedback that could have been helpful in enhancing his performance, the question may be raised as to why you violated your own policy in not issuing a timely performance appraisal. That question can be exacerbated if the employee in question claims a difference in treatment based on his membership in a protected class.

How

Objective rather than subjective documentation is another key. Let's say you have an administrative assistant who is making many errors. Telephone numbers in messages are transposed, records are misfiled, and typed memos are fraught with typographical or grammatical errors. An example of subjective documentation might be to write, "Your error rate is too high." Does that statement set the expectation? Does it tell the employee what the error rate should be? What is too high? You should also ensure the error rate is higher than the error rate of other employees in the same job classification who have not received comparable coaching or counseling.

What is the standard or acceptable error rate? Objective documentation quantifies the behavior being described. An example of objective documentation might be to write, "You are averaging 40 words per minute while the departmental average for administrative assistants is 55 words per minute." The same challenges and examples are often found when reviewing documentation related to attendance and punctuality. An employee is described as being "excessively" late or absent. But the reader has no idea what that means. Is the employee late an average of once per week or per month? Quantify, quantify, quantify. Soft skills can be a bit more difficult to quantify but you can attach measurable standards to them as well. How do you objectively document an employee's poor customer service skills? Perhaps you measure customer service by the number of customer complaints. So instead of telling an employee, "You need to improve your customer service skills," which is subjective and for which the employee may have no idea what you expect, you might say, "I expect to receive zero complaints regarding your customer service skills over the next 30 days."

Also be sure that you have communicated the expectation to the employee in advance. Do not wait until the employee has failed to meet your expectations to then tell the employee what that expectation is. Be proactive. Make it a part of your departmental orientation process to tell employees your departmental as well as job-specific expectations (see chapter 8). A departmental orientation could include not just an orientation to the employee's particular job and related duties but to your departmental expectations including but not limited to things like dress code, telephone use, attendance, and punctuality standards.

Why

Sometimes we wonder, "Why do I have to go through all this? Shouldn't an employee know what kind of attire is unprofessional and that he should come to work every day and on time?" While some may think the answer is "Yes," work environments vary much more today than they did 20 years ago. Dress codes, for example, range from professional to business casual to casual, and how employers define each of those also varies. The definition of proper workplace attire can vary dramatically from industry to industry, as well as between companies within the same industry. With the advent of flexible work schedules and styles like telecommuting, the lines have blurred with regard to "attending" work in the office as compared to attending from home. For example, some companies no longer offer paid leave; they focus, instead, on productivity regardless of the hours (not) worked. This is known as a Results-Oriented Work Environment (ROWE).[1]

Even methods of communicating have varied. I had a conversation with a manager who was frustrated because he felt the employee was not only absent and late frequently but the employee would send a text message to his manager instead of calling the manager by telephone directly. The manager acknowledged that he had never set an express expectation that employees notify him of an absence or lateness by telephone. The manager acknowledged that text messaging may seem quite acceptable to some but it was not to him. Lesson learned? Don't assume, be clear, and let your employees know in advance what is expected of them.

Making the Most of Performance Appraisals

There are a variety of terms used for various strategies employers use to provide feedback to employees regarding their performance. The term "performance appraisal" is often used interchangeably with "performance evaluation" and "performance review." For our purposes, we will consider these terms to refer to the same process: a periodic assessment of one or more aspects of an employee's work performance that is documented in writing, by one or more persons, including the employee's immediate supervisor, and is shared with the employee orally or in writing.

Performance Management Versus Performance Development

These terms are broader than performance appraisal. Performance management may refer to a broad, umbrella term used to describe an entire array of activities in which an employer may engage to maintain employees' work performance at a desire level and quality. This may include orientation, coaching, counseling, correcting, appraising, training, and more.

Performance development is one aspect of performance management by which the employer may provide sources for growing, advancing, and/or enhancing individual or team knowledge, skills, or abilities. This is often a part of succession planning, mentoring, and job shadowing programs.

For purposes of this book, we will consider performance appraisals to be tools by which an employer attempts to manage employee performance.

To Pay or Not to Pay—For Performance

Extensive research has been conducted to assess the pros and cons of associating pay increases with the results of performance appraisals. I find the results mixed. Some studies indicate that the two should be tied together;

others indicate they should be separate — that while it may be beneficial to tie compensation to performance it should not be tied to the performance appraisal process. For example, one study indicated that performance effectiveness is higher when financial rewards are tied to performance appraisal results. One 11-year survey of more than 200 companies indicated that in terms of financial and operational measures, companies with performance-enhancing cultures significantly outperformed companies without such cultures. In the same survey, 86 percent of the organizations reported tying bonus pay, at least in part, to individual performance.[2]

SHRM has gathered a variety of articles, resources, and tools employers may consider before implementing a new or modifying an existing process.[3]

Who

There is a wide variety of performance appraisal processes from which to choose. Who participates is just one factor that varies among some of these. There are at least two components to this question: Who will participate as a rater, appraiser, or evaluator, and who will participate as the person being rated? Let us consider the former first.

Most everyone is familiar with the traditional appraisal process by which an employee's manager or supervisor gives the employee a written performance appraisal. In this process the employee tends to be fairly passive, receiving the feedback, commenting, but usually without any formal documentation being required as a part of the process.

The next step may be to add a self-appraisal component. This often provides the employee with a form that is nearly identical to the form the manager completes and by which the employee can appraise his own performance using the same factors and the same rating scale as the manager. The two then meet, compare their responses, and hopefully engage in an interactive dialogue comparing and contrasting their respective responses. The manager retains the final say as to what actual ratings the employee receives but the self-appraisal can become a part of the official record and may be placed in the employee's HR file along with the manager's appraisal of the employee. This process more actively engages the employee and can help the manager better understand the employee's perception of his performance.

Peer reviews are used less frequently. When they are used, I find more often than not that they are used in particular industries such as health care or human services. In this process, not only does the employee's manager complete an appraisal of the employee's performance but so do some or all of the employee's peers. The results may be shared in a peer review meeting or individual results may be compiled into an average composite and shared with the employee in a one-on-one meeting with the employee's manager.

The most inclusive process may be the 360-degree appraisal process by which the employee's performance is appraised by the employee, the manager, the employee's peers, and the employee's direct reports (if any). Sometimes clients or customers are included in this process as well. The results are generally computerized or compiled into a composite result that compares overall ratings from each group with the overall ratings of the other groups. This gives the employee insight as to how his self-perception of his performance compares to that of his manager, peers, direct reports, and/or clients and customers. More often than not, this process is not tied to compensation but is used as a performance development tool.

But who in your organization will be appraised using your company's tool and process? Everyone? Staff only? Staff and managers? Executives? In a survey assessing the use of written performance plans, which are sometimes more detailed than performance appraisals, 70 percent of the respondents indicated they use written performance plans for executives; 64 percent did so for exempt employees, and 45 percent did so for non-exempt employees.[4] In other words, there is no "right" answer. Work backwards (like this book). Ask yourself what the company's goals are in using the performance appraisal process; why are you doing it? The answer to that question will likely be a good first step in determining who should or should not be included in the process.

What

What factors or behaviors should be appraised or evaluated? The answer to this question, as with many, may be best provided by the organization.

Getting feedback from focus groups that include executive team members, middle and front-line managers, as well as staff, is one strategy. This can be proactive and helpful in capturing the common and key factors and behaviors that your organization thinks are critical to successful performance, both individual and operational. For example, in a marketing firm, creativity may be highly valued and an important component of every employee's job as the business strives to create new and appealing ads for its clients. In manufacturing, however, where quality control requires zero deviation by employees working on the assembly line, creativity may not be desired and might actually be a hindrance to satisfactory work performance.

Another strategy is to develop a performance appraisal template. The core template can include sections for behaviors common to and expected of all employees, such as attendance, punctuality, work performance (what you do), and conduct (how you go about doing it). Depending upon the industry, you might add a section for safety as well. But the section related to work performance, which includes the employee's duties and responsibilities, may be different for each job title and mirrors the essential functions for any particular job.

No matter what strategy you use, it will be important to focus on what is important to your company's successful performance and develop corresponding behavioral and objective measures for that performance. For example, rather than rating an administrative assistant as to how well the employee "Completes projects in a timely manner," rate the employee using objective measures such as "Completes projects as scheduled at least 90 percent of the time." Another option is to keep the question as is and use a rating scale that quantifies the performance. See the next section on "How" for an example.

Finally, you can develop the very best tool, but if there is no accountability built into your process, it is less likely to succeed. Are your managers held accountable for not just completing performance appraisals for each of their employees but for completing them in a timely manner? If so, how? You could do so, for example, by including timely completion of performance appraisals as a behavior to be rated on each appraisal form that is to be used to appraise managers' performance. Example: "Completes 100 percent of the assigned performance appraisals in a timely manner (within 30 days of the due date) in the last year?"

How

I have mentioned "rating" several times throughout this section. But what does that mean? Performance can be appraised using a numerical scale, narrative format, or a combination of the two. The latter seems to be a common market practice. Managers may rate employee performance on a scale of 1 to 4, 1 to 5, or some other range. But which scale should you use and what does each represent? Even-numbered scales, like 1 to 4 or 1 to 10, are forced-choice scales; the rater is forced to rate the individual slightly above or slightly below the mid-point or "average." There is no middle-of-the-road. Some prefer this scale because it avoids the error of central tendency (read on; it's coming up under the section on Errors and Biases). Others dislike it because it cannot accurately reflect the performance of an employee who is truly performing at just a satisfactory level and meeting expectations. Thus, the latter may prefer to use an odd-numbered scale such as 1 to 5 that does provide a mid-point and reflects performance that is satisfactory and meets all expectations, not slightly above or below that middle level. Opponents of this methodology are concerned this may lead to the error of central tendency in which the manager might take the easy route and just mark everyone right down the middle of the scale, giving little thought to the process.

Once you have selected the areas of performance to be appraised (what) and the scale to be used (how), you might next consider whether or not the performance areas will be weighted equally. For example, let's say you rate performance in the four areas: (1) attendance/punctuality; (2) conduct/attitude; (3) performance of job duties; and (4) safety. A manufacturing company might weight safety slightly higher than conduct/attitude so that it accounts for 30 percent of an employee's overall rating, conduct/attitude account for 20 percent, and the other two areas account for 25 percent each.

As for including a narrative portion of feedback exclusively or in combination with a numerical scale, ensure participants are trained in writing objectively rather than subjectively. As described earlier in this chapter, for example, if a manager writes, "Christine's productivity is below average," do we really know at what level the employee is performing or where she should be? And based on what average, departmental? By job? Organizationally? A clearer appraisal might read, "Christine's average weekly productivity is 100 calls per week; that is the lowest in the department and 20 percent below the departmental average of 125 calls per week." Also consider including as a part of your performance appraisal process a step that includes an opportunity for review, such as by human resources, before the final appraisal is placed in the employee's file. This can provide one more perspective to help ensure goals and comments are written objectively and rating errors or rating biases are avoided. In one survey, 42 percent of the respondents indicated that senior management did not review any performance appraisals; 19 percent indicated that the HR department did not review any performance evaluations.[5]

Types of Appraisals

Before implementing or updating your appraisal process, research it. See what others in your industry are doing. The following is a list of some options you have when choosing an appraisal process[6] (some have been briefly described in this chapter already):

360/Multi-Rater

This involves a process by which information is collected from the employee's supervisor, colleagues, and subordinates about an individual's work-related behavior and its impact. Other names for this approach include multi-rater feedback, multi-source feedback, or group review. This form of appraisal is widely favored for employee development purposes.

Behaviorally Anchored Rating Systems

The behaviorally anchored rating systems (BARS) process attempts to assess employee behavior rather than specific characteristics. The appraisal tool generally contains a set of specific behaviors that represent gradations of performance and are used as common reference points, called "anchors," for rating employees on various job dimensions. Developing a BARS assessment tool is time-consuming and can be expensive because it is based on extensive job analysis and the collection of critical incidents for each specific job.

Competency-Based

This type of a system focuses on performance as measured against specified competencies (knowledge, skills, and abilities or KSAs) as opposed to specific tasks or behaviors that are identified for each position.

Forced Distribution

In this process the ratings of employees in a particular group are disbursed along a bell-shaped curve, with the supervisor allocating a certain percentage of the ratings within the group to each performance level on the scale. The actual distribution of employee performance may not actually resemble a bell curve, so supervisors may be forced to include some employees at either end of the scale when they would otherwise place them somewhere in the middle.

Graphic Rating Scales

Because of its simplicity, graphic rating scales (GRS) tends to be one of the most frequently used forms of performance appraisal. These appraisals list a number of factors, including general behaviors and characteristics (e.g., attendance, dependability, quality of work, quantity of work, and relationships with people) on which a supervisor rates an employee. The rating is usually based on a scale of three to five gradations (e.g., unsatisfactory, marginal, satisfactory, highly satisfactory, and outstanding). This type of system allows the rater to determine the performance of an employee along a continuum.

Management by Objectives

Management by objectives (MBO) is a process through which goals are set collaboratively for the organization as a whole, various departments, and each individual member. Employees are evaluated annually based on how well they have achieved the results specified by the goals. MBO is particularly applicable to non-routine jobs, such as those of managers, project leaders, and individual contributors.

Peer Review

This process is less comprehensive than but similar to the 360 assessment process. It involves collecting information from the employee's peers only about an individual's work-related behavior and its impact. Like the 360, this form of appraisal may be used for employee development purposes.

Ranking

This process consists of listing all employees in a designated group from highest to lowest in order of performance. The primary drawback is that quantifying the differences in individual performance is difficult and may involve drawing very narrow — if not meaningless — distinctions. It may also skew results where an entire team is low-performing but, by definition, must rank someone as a top performer of the group.

***

There are many options, and learning more about each will help you make the best decision as to the right "fit" for your organization.

A final note on "how" would be about training. So often employees or managers are given a blank appraisal form and told to complete it. It seems pretty straightforward, right? You will recall that I mentioned using feedback from focus groups to develop your appraisal tool, including feedback from staff. You may find there are many components of the performance appraisal process of which your staff and managers are not aware or do not understand: "How does the appraisal affect my pay?" "What if I don't agree, can I put something in my HR file?" "What if I don't get my annual appraisal?" "What if my employee won't complete the self-appraisal form?"

One of my (several) memorable lessons from when I was in HR administration was with an employee who was at the end of her probationary period (yes, this was a union environment so we had a probationary period rather than an introductory period). She received a low rating for attendance and punctuality. One of her complaints was, "If I had known attendance and punctuality were weighted so high I wouldn't have been late so much." While that recollection makes me smile to this day, and I still think it was not a very good excuse for excessive lateness, it was a teachable moment for us as the employer. We failed to set the expectation for that employee from day one. (Of course now I must refer you to chapter 3.) From that point on we included a blank copy of our performance appraisal in the new hire packet and incorporated a brief overview of the performance appraisal process in our new employee orientation program (see chapter 8).

And don't forget your managers. Train them with the same core information you provide to employees. Help prepare them for likely employee responses, such as managing emotional reactions (see chapter 3); what your company's process is for rebuttals (*can* an employee put a written response in his HR file or file a grievance?); information on common rating errors and biases so they can avoid them by being aware of them (see next section); and more.

Rating Errors and Rating Biases

Search the employment headlines and it is not hard to find a reference to performance appraisals being used by the plaintiff as evidence of discrimination. Not because the employee received a poor rating, just the opposite: The employee received an exemplary rating and shortly thereafter was terminated for unsatisfactory work performance.

All too often, it may seem easier to go ahead and give an employee a satisfactory rating on a performance appraisal rather than managing the potential conflict and emotional reactions that can come with telling an employee that his performance is sub-par. Instead, be candid, and be objective. The following are some common rating errors or biases that you should keep in mind and avoid when completing performance appraisals.

Halo Effect

This results when we unintentionally permit an employee's competency in one area to overshadow incompetency in other areas. I see this happen more often than not in technical or sales positions. You may have heard of the "Peter Principle" developed by Dr. Laurence J. Peter and Raymond Hull in their classic book, *The Peter Principle*, which maintains that employees tend to rise to their level of incompetence.[7] How? Employers promote them to that level. Why? Sometimes we want to reward a top performer, such as an employee who is technically savvy or makes a lot of sales or brings in lots of new clients. So we promote the person to a team leader, supervisor, manager, and/or director. In that process we may not have given sufficient thought to the person's management skills (or lack thereof). Next thing you know, the person is no longer performing any of the technical, sales or business development work at which he was so good. Now he is managing people with no clue as to how to do so efficiently.

Primacy Effect

This is the tendency to let the first impression overshadow other, subsequent behavior. Have you ever had a star employee and then wondered what happened the day after the introductory or probationary period was over? The person shined and then as soon as he felt he was "in" the sheen began to dull. Sometimes we become so enamored with our new star employee that we fail to see the slow decline in performance and continue to see the employee as he was in that honeymoon stage of the employment relationship. You can avoid this by making periodic reviews of work performance and focusing on quality, quantity, attendance, punctuality, etc. Checking these for all your employees on at least a quarterly basis can help you proactively monitor performance and prevent the company and coworkers from being burdened with an individual who is no longer carrying his share of the workload.

Error of Central Tendency

This occurs when we rate all employees within a narrow range regardless of differences in individual performance. This may be the result of an attempt to avoid conflict. Rather than taking the time to distinguish the high from the low performers a manager may simply rate all employees as satisfactory. It may be faster and easier in the short run but not when you need an accurate performance appraisal to substantiate your need to terminate an employee for poor performance; having an unrealistic, satisfactory appraisal can work against you. This rating error more frequently occurs when using odd-numbered rating scales such as 1 to 5.

Recency Effect

This is the tendency to let the last event overshadow prior behaviors. Sometimes this is the case when a very recent event, positive or negative, has occurred and is overshadowing your recollection of the employee's prior performance. Something recently went very awry and is wiping out your recollection of all the good work the employee has done over the last year. Or the employee just did a great job such as inventing a new process that will reduce costs and generate revenue for the company and you are discounting his lack of performance over the last year. Again, this is where your informal documentation can help you recall the quality of work and related issues that have arisen over time.

Leniency Error

This error occurs when we rate all employees favorably to avoid giving low marks. This error may have the greatest potential to fiscally impact your budget. This may happen, not so much to avoid conflict, but when a manager feels everyone is trying to do his best despite the fact that productivity, quality, or other factors are not being met. When creating your labor budget for the upcoming fiscal year, you generally project wage increases, if any, assuming a bell shaped curve. For example, a company offers something other than cost-of-living adjustments (COLA) such as some type of merit pay or pay for performance increase. When projecting increases for next year's budget, they may assume that most employees will fall into the middle with some outliers falling at the far ends of the performance spectrum with some high and some low performers. When this error is applied across several departments and wage increases are tied to performance evaluation ratings, it unexpectedly skews the results to the right of that bell-shaped curve, costing your company more money than budgeted because higher ratings equal higher pay increases.

Remember that performance appraisals are (or should be) tied to the job duties and responsibilities, not the person. If someone is trying his best but still cannot meet job expectations, then they are not satisfactorily fulfilling the responsibilities of that job. Perhaps the selection was not a good match; e.g., it was a poor hire or the employee has not been provided with adequate training. Whatever the case, you must be candid in your assessment and determine what you can provide that employee, if anything, to enable him to meet those expectations.

When

Like so many factors in this process, it is up to you to decide when and how frequently your company will conduct performance appraisals. A common practice is annually upon each employee's anniversary date. Employers that have an introductory period often conduct a performance evaluation at the end of that period as well. As I mentioned earlier, be sure you define the term "annually" so employees know what to expect and when. Do you mean appraisals will be conducted on a calendar year basis, fiscal year basis, or on the employee's anniversary date? Smaller organizations may choose to appraise all employees at the same time and use the start or end of the calendar or fiscal year. As companies grow in size, this may become burdensome as they would have to appraise hundreds of employees at the same time. Instead, they may choose to use employees' anniversary dates. Whatever date(s) you choose, ensure they are completed in a timely manner, and define "timely" so your managers know what is expected of them as well. As mentioned at the start of this chapter, not only do inaccurate performance appraisals have the potential to create legal turmoil but the absence of an appraisal for one employee when others have received theirs may also give the appearance of adverse treatment.

Practical Tips

- My father often said to me, "Do it right or don't do it at all." That lesson has served me well over the years. The thought is the same in the common phrase, "A job worth doing is worth doing well." This is probably the third time I have alluded to this concept in this chapter but it is very important; if you have a performance appraisal program, process, and/or policy, then be sure to follow it. Don't spend the time and energy in forming focus groups; developing tools, systems and processes; running pilot programs; and more if you are not going to hold employees and managers accountable for actively participating in the process.

- Set the expectation from day one; consider including a blank appraisal form in your new hire packet so employees can see, in advance, how and on what their performance will be appraised.

- Incorporate a quick review of the appraisal form and process into your new employee orientation program or onboarding process (see chapter 8).

- Provide training for your staff and managers to anticipate their questions, and provide answers and practical tips for making the process easier.

- Anticipate challenges: Consider whether or not you want to include a signature line at the end of the appraisal form for the employee to sign. If so, how will you handle an employee who declines to sign? Consider including a statement that indicates that the employee's signature displays that he has received the appraisal and does not necessarily indicate that he agrees with the appraisal.

- Here's a tip from when I was in human resources: We had approximately 3,500 employees and keeping up with the ever-changing job descriptions (health care industry) was becoming overwhelming for the HR staff and our management team members. To help us all stay on track, we added a question on the employees' self-appraisal form to the effect, "Does your current job description fairly and accurately describe your current duties and responsibilities? Yes/ No." If the employee checked "No," that was a flag for human resources when we received the final copy of the completed appraisal to contact the employee's manager, get his feedback, and discuss the need for a desk audit or informal review to update the job description along with the employee's input.

3

Coaching, Counseling, and Correcting

Writer and psychiatrist Theodore Rubin said, "The problem is not that there are problems. The problem is expecting otherwise and thinking that having problems is a problem."[1]

Whether your role is as an HR administrator, business owner, manager, or supervisor, you are also the complaint department. Your job is to take employees' complaints. And you know what? You should be thankful for nearly every complaint you receive. Why? It takes trust. Employees generally will not complain to someone they do not trust. So the next time an employee comes to you with a complaint, smile. Be thankful that they are complaining to you and not an external agency. Take it as a compliment; you are trusted.

In chapter 6 we will "talk" about the basic nature of the employment relationship and at-will employment. But for now, let's ask, "If employment is at-will, why bother with coaching, counseling, and/or correcting? Why can't I just let an employee go?" Well, basically you can (unless you are doing business in a state like Montana that does not recognize at-will employment), assuming your reason for terminating the employee does not establish some form of unlawful discrimination or retaliation, or have some other unlawful basis. So why *should* you coach, counsel, or correct prior to termination? That takes a lot of time and energy. But consider this. How much time, money, and energy have you already spent just bringing this person on board? Add up your advertising dollars, lower productivity during the learning curve, plus your time in recruiting, interviewing, selecting, and hiring — you have made a substantial investment in this individual. Do you really want to toss that aside and start all over again?

So, if we agree that there is a valid return on investment (ROI) in coaching, counseling, and correcting, then let's begin.

Coaching

What nouns and adjectives come to mind when you think of a coach? Trainer, teacher, instructor, mentor, and more? At what point do you begin setting expectations for your new employees? The first day of employment? During new employee orientation? How about during the employment interview? What better time to let a prospective employee know what you expect in your department, not to mention the organization as a whole? What is your expectation with regard to professional attire? Attendance and punctuality? Customer service?

And once the employee is on-board (see chapter 8), how do you practically set expectations? Be specific: "I expect employees in my department to be punctual, and we do not tolerate excessive absenteeism." Does the employee know what you really expect? How is punctuality defined? Some people would say one minute late is late; others would say it depends on the job; while others would say a few minutes is no big deal. How do you define excessive absenteeism? Does the reason for the absence make a difference? What if it was scheduled in advance, would that count in your definition of excessive? Don't assume. While you know what you mean you cannot assume that the employee does. Be clear and specific: "I expect employees in my department to have no more than one unscheduled late day and no more than one unscheduled absence each month."

Many times employees become frustrated because they thought they followed a supervisor's instruction only to learn that they had not. Clear communication of expectations is a shared responsibility. You cannot assume an employee knows what you mean when you use descriptive verbs like increase, decrease, improve. Quantify, quantify, quantify. And use time tables to set your expectations. I suspect most every person reading this book has heard the acronym for giving "SMART" instructions or directions. You may have heard it before but I believe it is worth repeating and giving due consideration with practical examples. I must say before proceeding, I have found no less than eight variations of the acronym and suspect it depends upon the author you are reading;[2] most variations, however, focus on similar principles.

Specific

When you give an employee an instruction, be sure it is specific, such as including behavioral examples. Rather than telling an employee, "You are expected to always provide quality customer service" you might say, "You are expected to greet every customer with 'Good morning' or 'Good afternoon' and ask, 'How may I help you?'"

Measurable

Where possible, use behavioral objectives that can be measured. Rather than telling an employee, "You are expected to maintain consistently high quality with a low error rate," you might say, "You are expected to maintain consistently high quality by producing an average error rate of no more than two percent." As mentioned in the previous chapter, I find one of the most challenging aspects of this element arises when dealing with soft skills, such as described above; how do you measure quality customer service? Even that can be quantified by telling an employee, "We expect no customer service representative to receive more than one customer complaint per quarter."

Attainable or Achievable

An employee cannot succeed in performing your assigned task if he does not have the requisite knowledge, skills, and abilities (KSA) to accomplish the task. Be sure your employee has been trained in how to do a task before expecting him to perform it. I remember a time when I was in human resources in a hospital and an employee who worked in the operating room was written up for violating the department's sterile protocol. Without going into all the detail, in short, he had not laid out the instruments the way the surgeon and department expected and had inadvertently contaminated the sterile field. His explanation was that he laid out the instruments as he was taught in medical school. Further research revealed that there were, in fact, different approaches as to how a sterile field could be established. What a teachable moment. The department needed to ensure they taught employees as to the protocol they wanted employees to follow rather than assuming that everyone followed the same protocol.

Realistic

I distinguish this factor from the one above as extrinsic versus intrinsic. An employee may have the intrinsic KSAs to get the job done but may be constrained by extrinsic factors such as not having the authority to get the job done; thus it is not realistic for the employee to be able to accomplish what you ask. Take the example of an inventory supply clerk who lets inventory levels fall below par. The employee's explanation is that he did know how, when, and from whom to order the supplies. He could not do so, however, because he was authorized to order only up to $200 of inventory. The needed supplies cost $500 and the purchasing agent who could authorize this order was on vacation. This employee was not given the resource nor was he empowered with the authority he needed to get the job done. Yes, there is still accountability on the employee's part for not taking this a step further and asking his supervisor for assistance, but this problem was created as a result of a shared responsibility on the employer's part as well.

Timely

This is a common pitfall that I see frustrate employees time and time again. A manager gives an employee a task but fails to provide a timeline. When the manager subsequently asks the employee why the task has not been completed the employee replies, "I was going to get it done next week; I did not know you wanted it done sooner!" Be sure to tell your employee when you want a task completed and when you might check on his interim progress. Employees may feel micromanaged if they are given an assignment with a 30-day window and the manager checks in every week asking, "How is it coming along?" While the manager may feel he is being supportive, the employee may feel the manager does not trust him. Tell your employee, in advance, not only when the task should be completed but that you may check in on him on a weekly basis in the interim. That way the expectation is set and no one should be surprised or frustrated by periodic checks.

Counseling

Now that you have set objective and measureable expectations, what if the employee is not meeting them? How can you best redirect behavior? Once again, focus on measurable performance standards. In addition, use the following tips to help the employee understand the importance of the task and the result if outcomes are not achieved.

Manage the "What" Versus the "How"

Your job is to tell employees what to do; you direct, supervise, instruct, train, staff, schedule, and more. You are responsible for overseeing what employees do. However, you may not have to so closely manage how they do it. Of course the how is critical in certain industries. How a nurse pushes a syringe into a patient to administer medication is critical, but whether an administrative assistant produces a financial report in Access™ or Excel™ may not be critical so long as the data that is needed is provided. Let go! Empower your employees. Have you ever been frustrated as a customer when the clerk waiting on you does not have the authority to do what you ask and it seems like such a simple thing? You want to return an item you purchased, perhaps. You don't want your money back; you only want to exchange the product for another one of a different color. The clerk tells you he is not authorized to make exchanges — only the manager can do that. So you have to stand around and wait 10 minutes until the manager finishes with another customer. Then you find all the manager does is walk over to you, ask what you want, and hand you the item of your choice. A 60-second transaction took you 10 minutes to complete because the clerk was not empowered to do this for you. Everybody loses. You lost time, the clerk lost the ability to help you, and the store may have lost you as a customer. Lesson learned? Try to not micro-manage your employees. Empower them as much as possible. Let go!

Ask "How" Before "Who"

When something goes wrong, what is the first question we often ask? "Who did it?" is often the first question we ask. While that is an important question, consider making that the second question you ask. Consider making your first question, "How did that happen?" Are there certain protocols, checks, and balances that are not in place that should be? Then ask, "Who?" as an important second question to ensure the employee(s) involved has the required knowledge, skills, and abilities to perform the assigned tasks.

"I" Versus "You" Statements

How often do we tell others what they have (have not) done without really knowing the facts? Have you ever called a customer service department and been told, "You dialed the wrong number." Then, when you repeat the number you dialed, the person on the other end of the line tells you, "Oh, that's the right number; I guess they transferred their extension over here." Or how about e-mail or voice mail? Has anyone ever told you, "Hey, you never answered my e-mail message," or "Hey, you never called me back after I left you a voice mail message," when, in fact, you did reply but their inbox was full and would not accept any more messages. From these day-to-day experiences we learn that it may be better to use "I" rather than "You." The same applies to managing your employees. Rather than telling your employee what he did or did not do, tell the employee what you do or do not have. For example, "I don't have the report from you that I requested to have by close of business yesterday." This gives the employee the opportunity to tell you what he did or did not do without getting frustrated because you have made an inappropriate assumption. For example, he might tell you that he did put the report in your inbox at 3:00 p.m. yesterday and there is now so much stuff on top of it that you did not see it.

Why You Do What You Do

Have you ever been frustrated and wondered why an employee was not getting it? Maybe you have talked to the employee once, twice, and maybe even a third time about the same performance problem. Ask yourself this: Having told the employee what (and what not) to do, when was the last time you told the employee why it needs to be done or why it is important? Adult learning theory contends, among many things, that adult learners seek to understand why:[3] we strive to practically apply theory; it is not enough for us to just know what to do, we seek to understand why it should be done. Empowered employees more often than not understand how what they do contributes to the operations of the business, its mission, and more because they have been told why they do what they do. For example, a pharmacy aide is repeatedly told that he must get certain medications into the medication cart no later than 8:00 a.m. Invariably, he repeatedly gets the medications into the cart between 8:10 and 8:15. The employee is frustrated and thinks his boss is a pain and a control freak. What's the big deal? It's just 5 or 10 minutes! What the manager has never told the employee are the implications of those few minutes. What the employee does not know is that the medications are used in surgery and are picked up everything 30 minutes at five and 35 minutes after the hour. So when this employee delivers the medications at 10 or 15 minutes after the hour, they will not be picked up for another 20 to 25 minutes and surgery may have to be delayed. This can have a critical and adverse outcome for the patient awaiting that surgery. If only the pharmacy aide had known the implications of his actions he might have taken greater care to be timely. But his manager never told him why, just what.

Speak Up!

How about this scenario: Have you ever been so frustrated with an employee's unsatisfactory performance that instead of giving him more work or new assignments you have just done the work yourself or reassigned them to a coworker? If you do that and say nothing to the employee, how will he learn? How will he know that his performance is unsatisfactory? Your silence may reasonably be interpreted as condoning the unsatisfactory conduct. Not to mention the frustration that a coworker may feel at having to do another employee's work. Remember the 80-20 rule or the Pareto Principle?[4] It has many applications and basically holds that 80 percent of the effects or results come from 20 percent of the causes. Applied to the workplace, examples include the premise that you spend 80 percent of your time on 20 percent of your employees or 20 percent of your employees complete 80 percent of the work. Here you may be fostering the latter rule. Why? You have designed it that way by redistributing work assignments. Thus the rule has become a self-fulfilling prophecy. Do not let that happen. You have a responsibility to expressly tell the employee, whether you think he should know better or not, that the performance level is not meeting expectations. You owe that to yourself, the employee, and the coworkers.

Correcting

So now you are at the point at which you have coached and counseled, and still the employee's performance is not meeting expectations. You have concluded it is time to issue corrective action. Here are a few things to consider.

Corrective Versus Disciplinary Action

You may notice I used the term corrective action rather than disciplinary action. I find the latter term still used in many employee handbooks. Neither term is good or bad nor right or wrong. I prefer corrective action because it focuses on the purpose of the action rather than on the person. It emphasizes the purpose, which is to correct behavior or to entice the employee to start or stop doing something. Disciplinary action may be read as a punitive term and seems to focus more on the person; e.g., it is punishment of the individual for a job not well done. If you agree and your company uses the latter term in its employee handbook, you might replace "discipline" and "disciplinary action" with "corrective action" next time you update your handbook. It's funny in a way. Sometimes a manager may ask me, usually after an employee has been coached and counseled multiple times and is being offered one last chance prior to termination, "But what if I issue discipline and the employee improves?" Isn't that the point?

Equal Versus Equitable Treatment

This topic was addressed in chapter 1, but we will revisit it here. Have you ever had an employee tell you that your corrective action was unfair because the employee knows someone else who did the same thing but did not get "written up"? I suspect we all have. First, you know that it is quite likely that you did write the other employee up but this employee just does not know about it, as it should be. Second, and more to the point here, is that even if that is the case — e.g., another employee did do the same thing and did not get written up — so what? This is the difference between equal and equitable treatment. Most managers do not want to treat all their employees exactly the same nor do most employees want to be treated the same as all others, especially your top performers. What rising star wants to work under a compensation system that provides cost of living adjustments (COLA) only and get the same pay increase as everyone else? What employee wants to be written up for excessive lateness when he is caring for a terminally ill child or family member (exclusive of FMLA leave, of course)? Treating employees equitably requires wise use of management discretion. It takes into account all the factors that come into play in any given scenario. At the risk of repeating from chapter 1, take two employees who have both had 10 separate and unscheduled occurrences of absence in the last six months. You may not want to issue both employees the same level of corrective action if

(1) one employee has been with you for 10 years, has an exemplary performance record, and all 10 absences have been to provide care for a terminally ill family member (forget FMLA for purposes of this example; if you can't, then read chapter 4); and

(2) the other employee has been with you for just over one year, has documented marginal performance, and most of the absences have been for a variety of personal reasons.

You may decide to not treat these employees equally; you may issue corrective action to one and not the other. But that may not be inequitable because the two employees are not similarly situated.

Let me take a moment here to share some responses to the question above. What do you say when an employee tells you that you are not being fair because a coworker did the same thing and did not get written up? This might happen in the investigatory phase, as you are meeting with the employee to get his side of the story. Or you might hear it for the first time when you issue corrective action or give the employee anything less than an "Excellent" rating on his performance appraisal. How do you respond? I find a common response is "We're here to talk about you, not your coworker." That is true but does not leave you open to a full investigation of all the facts. I prefer a response that lets the employee know that you heard him, will consider what he shared, and then redirects the employee back to the conversation at hand: "I hear that you think it's not fair because Christine did the same thing and I will look into that and address that with her if that is the case. For now, I want to focus on my expectations for you."

Regardless of what you call it, corrective action is generally formal in nature in that it involves a writing of some type that is placed in the employee's HR file. Some companies use a standard form that managers fill out; others simply use a memo-style approach. In either case, the written document then becomes a part of the employment record.

Employee Acknowledgement

I find a common question is whether the employer should provide a space for and/or require the employee to sign an acknowledgement that the employee has received the written notice of corrective action. There are some advantages and disadvantages regardless of which method you decide to use. Here is a brief, comparative review.

If you do not have a signature line for the employee to indicate his receipt of the form, you may create the opportunity for the employee to later claim, such as at an unemployment insurance (UI) or other administrative agency hearing, that the employee was never notified that he was not meeting expectations. You might overcome this by having a practice of always having another management-level witness present whenever you issue written, corrective action. The disadvantage of witnesses is that the employee could feel as if you were "ganging up" on him or not respecting the privacy of this "teachable moment." The decision of whether or not to have a witness is best made by you. You know your individual employees and for whom you are more likely than not to want a witness present. If you decide to not have a witness and also no signature, then you will bear the burden to show that the employee did, in fact, receive your written notice.

But having a signature line is not all a bed of roses either. How often have you had an employee refuse to sign? I suspect you are nodding yes right now. This is not uncommon. If the employee does not agree with the content or level of the corrective action, he may be inclined to not sign. Again, there is a strategy you might use to overcome this objection. For instance, on the performance appraisals, you may have a statement under the signature line that reads that the employee's signature does not necessarily indicate agreement with the notice but simply acknowledges his receipt of the notice. Still, even with that disclaimer, employees may still decline to sign the form.

This leads to the third issue as to whether the employer should make the signature a requirement of the corrective action or an option. I prefer the latter as it is usually better received by the employee. In this case, if the employee does not want to sign, the manager may simply write, "Employee declined to sign." I also prefer "declined" rather than "Employee refused to sign." The former is less confrontational. The offer to sign is an invitation, not a mandate, so the employee has the option to accept or decline your invitation to sign.

Managing Emotional Reactions

In any of these steps, particularly counseling and correcting, an employee may respond with one or more emotional reactions. Here are some tips for effectively managing your response to some of the more common emotional reactions.

Anger

Sometimes an employee may become angry when confronted with counseling on performance deficiencies. Your reaction can help de-escalate that emotion. Don't get drawn into the moment; watch the pace, pitch, and volume of your own voice (PPV). The PPV of an angry person's voice usually increases; they speak faster, at a higher pitch, and louder. Sometimes it can help to de-escalate this emotional reaction by doing just the opposite. Reduce the PPV of your own voice. Respond in a slow, low, and quiet tone of voice, such that the person may have to actually pause in his own frenetic pace of speech to listen to you. In that moment, you may recapture the person's attention and invite the person to take a break from the conversation and begin again in a few minutes or perhaps even in a few hours or the next day. At this point, the emotion may override any productivity that could be derived from the meeting. How effective can you be when the person is focused on his own anger? Give the person time to return to a calm state before re-engaging him in the conversation. On another note, keep yourself safe. (See chapter 5 for tips for avoiding certain legal claims like intentional infliction of emotional distress and false imprisonment, as well as keeping yourself safe from a potentially violent employee.)

Denial or Blaming

Have you ever counseled an employee only to hear him accept no responsibility and state that the fault is not his but someone else's? As mentioned above, sometimes we may be compelled to tell the person that we are not there to discuss a coworker but to discuss this employee's performance. But if a coworker really is the source of a problem, the employee may hear that you are brushing off his very valid complaint. It may be appropriate to tell the employee that you will address those concerns momentarily and to then ask, before you do so, what responsibility this employee has, if any, for the concerns you have shared with him. For example, you might ask, "I understand your concern and we can talk about that in a moment. Before we do, let me ask first, what could you have done differently in this situation to have avoided this problem?" That question may help keep the conversation focused on this employee before getting side tracked to other issues. The other reported issues, however, should be addressed so you can determine whether or not they are valid concerns.

Silence

Humorist Josh Billings said, "Silence is one of the hardest arguments to refute."[5] And isn't this the truth? How do you engage an employee in a productive conversation when all he does is nod, shrug, and give an occasional, "I dunno." You have probably heard about open- versus closed-ended questions. Here is a great time to try using open-ended questions. Rather than asking questions that can be answered with a "yes" or "no," ask questions that require a descriptive response. For example, a common question as we wrap up a meeting with an employee may be to ask, "Do you have any questions?" What does the employee almost always say? "No." Or you might ask, "Do you understand what I'm asking?" And, again, you get the closed-ended response, "Yes." But do you really know that the employee understands your expectations? An open-ended method for asking the same question would be to ask, "OK, just before wrap up, tell me what you understand my expectation to be." This cannot be answered with a "yes" or "no" but requires the employee to repeat what he understands you want him to do. If you still get silence or a shrug, then you have the opportunity to again share the expectation and then ask the employee again, in an open-ended way, to tell you what he understands the expectation to be.

Another strategy for overcoming silence can be to offer the employee the opportunity to share his thoughts in writing. Some people just are not good orators; they are not comfortable telling you what is bothering them but could do so in writing. You might offer the employee the opportunity to think about what you have shared overnight and provide you with a written response the next day or by the end of the week.

Tears

Whether they are crocodile tears or real tears, this emotional reaction can be awkward to manage. First tip: always have a box of tissues in your office. There are few moments more awkward than when a tearful employee has no recourse but to wipe his nose on his sleeve. Keep the tissue box on your desk, rather than in a drawer, so the employee can take one rather than having to ask for one. Like managing anger, it may also be best to give the employee 5 to 10 minutes to collect himself and then return to the conversation. The question here may be where do you or the employee go during this interim period? That depends upon your office location as well as what is in your office. If you are an HR administrator with confidential files in your office that are unlocked, it may be best to invite the employee to step out and get a drink of water and return rather than leaving the employee alone in your office with access to files. On the other hand, if your office is in a highly trafficked hallway, telling the person to step out into a public area for all to see that he has been crying might not be wise either. Give these points consideration; you may decide that a meeting is best held in a neutral area such as a small conference room or vacant office space. That way, if a break is needed, you can tell the employee that you will step out, give the employee time to compose himself, and then return to continue the meeting.

Tears may also indicate that the employee is dealing with an issue unrelated to work that is personal in nature. If your company has an employee assistance program (EAP), this is a wonderful opportunity to remind the employee of this confidential resource if they need or would like someone else to talk to about work or personal matters that may be impacting work performance. Why do I say confidential? Remember that your EAP counselor is usually either a licensed social worker (LSW) or licensed clinical social worker (LCSW). That license gives the counselor a legal veil of confidentiality such that what the employee tells that counselor (barring a threat to self or others) is truly confidential. The EAP counselor may not disclose the information shared by the employee with the employer without the employee's consent. You, however, cannot provide an employee with absolute confidentiality. If you do refer an employee to the EAP, put a note on your calendar to follow up with the employee in a week or two. Tell the employee that you will do so, and then check in with the employee to see how things are going.

Tread lightly, however, when referring an employee to the EAP. Don't let this offer create an opportunity for the employee to then disclose to you personal information that could later be used against you, such as disclosing that he is caring for a family member with a disability and is having trouble managing the related stress (the association provision of the Americans with Disabilities Act may now apply). If the employee does begin to disclose personal information, it may be best to redirect the conversation. Tell the employee that personal matters are best shared with the EAP counselor and the time you spend with the employee is best used to focus on performance issues.

Passive-Aggressive

This pattern of behavior may be less gently referred to as being two-faced. This behavior is demonstrated by the employee who is very reticent, polite, and apologetic in your presence, indicating he is sorry and will do better moving forward. After the employee leaves your office, however, you begin to hear from coworkers that he is complaining about you and the company, unfair treatment, and generally bad-mouthing the organization. What do you do? Ask the employee about it. You may simply tell him that it has come to your attention that he may be complaining about you or the company. Can you guess what the employee's first question often is? That's right, "Who told you that?" There is no need to disclose that to the employee. Notice that I indicated you would tell the employee that it has come to your attention that he "may be" complaining. You may simply tell him that who told you is not important; what is important is that he understands that such behavior is not acceptable. Remind the employee of the company's appropriate resources for expressing concerns (e.g., the employee's supervisor, human resources, EAP, confidential hotline). Then advise the employee that if you continue to receive such reports and you find that he is, in fact, engaging in such behavior, it may result in corrective action. Let him know that venting to coworkers and contaminating workplace morale is not acceptable. Here's another common question: "But doesn't that violate the employee's right to freedom of speech?" Remember that freedom of speech is a constitutional matter applicable only to the public sector or government employers, not the private sector. And for those of you reading this book and who work in the public sector, even the U.S. Supreme Court has held, "The first amendment does not require a public office to be run as a roundtable for employee complaints over internal office affairs."[6]

Practical Tips

- Why wait until the employee is onboard? Begin setting expectations in your job interviews; tell candidates about your company's culture, work ethic, core values and your general, departmental expectations.

- Don't presume understanding. Use the skills described in this chapter to ensure the employee understands your expectations. Give SMART instructions and ask open-ended questions.

- Don't procrastinate. I have seen it happen time and again when a manager puts off coaching, counseling, or correcting, and just before he finally decides to take some type of action, the employee expresses a need for FMLA leave or military leave, files a workers' compensation claim, or informs the employer she is pregnant — or something else happens that could now make the corrective action look like retaliation.

4

Employee, Where Art Thou? Managing Disability and Leave Issues

Who has not been frustrated at one time or another with an employee who is excessively late, absent, or seems to be missing too frequently from his work area? From smoke breaks, to personal telephone calls, to tardiness and absences, today's employees face challenges in balancing a variety of personal and professional demands, as do you. This chapter will focus on those issues that seem to give rise, more often than not, to litigation, as well as frustrated employee relations.

The Americans with Disabilities Act

On January 1, 2009, the Americans with Disabilities Act Amendments Act (ADAAA) took effect. This law amended the Americans with Disabilities Act (ADA) and expanded the coverage of protected individuals. The ADA now emphasizes that the definition of disability should be construed in favor of broad coverage of individuals to the maximum extent permitted by the terms of the ADA and generally shall not require extensive analysis.[1]

The Act made important changes to the definition of the term "disability" by rejecting the holdings in several Supreme Court decisions and portions of ADA regulations of the Equal Employment Opportunity Commission (EEOC). The effect of these changes is to make it easier for an individual seeking protection under the ADA to establish that he has a disability within the meaning of the ADA.

The Act retained the ADA's basic definition of "disability" as an impairment that substantially limits one or more major life activities, a record of such an impairment, or being regarded as having such an impairment. A substantial limitation is generally long-term or permanent. A broken leg that is expected to mend in eight weeks would not generally qualify as a disability. While the individual is certainly limited in major life activities while the leg is broken, it is of a relatively short term or duration. The Act does, however, change the way that these statutory terms should be interpreted in several ways. Most significantly, the Act:

- Directs EEOC to revise that portion of its regulations defining the term "substantially limits" (publication is pending as of this writing and expected sometime in 2010);

- Expands the definition of "major life activities" by including two non-exhaustive lists: the first list includes many activities that the EEOC has recognized (e.g., walking), as well as activities that EEOC has not specifically recognized (e.g., reading, bending, and communicating); the second list includes major bodily functions (e.g., "functions of the immune system, normal cell growth, digestive, bowel, bladder, neurological, brain, respiratory, circulatory, endocrine, and reproductive functions");

- States that mitigating measures other than "ordinary eyeglasses or contact lenses" shall not be considered in assessing whether an individual has a disability;

- Clarifies that an impairment that is episodic or in remission is a disability if it would substantially limit a major life activity when active;

- Changes the definition of "regarded as" so that it no longer requires a showing that the employer perceived the individual to be substantially limited in a major life activity, and instead says that an applicant or employee is "regarded as" disabled if he or he is subject to an action prohibited by the ADA (e.g., failure to hire or termination) based on an impairment that is not transitory and minor; and

- Provides that individuals covered only under the "regarded as" prong are not entitled to reasonable accommodation.

As of this writing the EEOC is evaluating the impact of these changes on its enforcement guidance and other publications addressing the ADA.[2]

The ADA still generally covers employers with 15 or more employees. In addition to the above, the law also prohibits discrimination against a qualified individual because of the known disability of an individual with whom the qualified individual is known to have a relationship or association. The ADA covers your current employees, former employees, and applicants. It is important to note that the law protects qualified individuals with disabilities. A qualified individual is one who can perform the essential functions of your job with or without a reasonable accommodation.

The law also requires a covered employer to provide a reasonable accommodation to a qualified individual with a disability. The federal regulations consider five elements to determine whether an accommodation is reasonable:

1. The nature and net cost of the accommodation needed, taking into consideration the availability of tax credits and deductions, and/or outside funding;

2. The overall financial resources of the facility or facilities involved in the provision of the reasonable accommodation, the number of persons employed at such facility, and the effect on expenses and resources;

3. The overall financial resources of the covered entity, the overall size of the business of the covered entity with respect to the number of its employees, and the number, type, and location of its facilities;

4. The type of operation or operations of the covered entity, including the composition, structure, and functions of the workforce of such entity, and the geographic separateness and administrative or fiscal

relationship of the facility or facilities in question to the covered entity; and

5. The impact of the accommodation upon the operation of the facility, including the impact on the ability of other employees to perform their duties and the impact on the facility's ability to conduct business.[3]

So, for example, a likely reasonable accommodation may be if an employee who worked on a loading dock needed a hydraulic hand jack that cost $70 to lift boxes weighing more than 50 pounds up to and down from the loading platform. If the employee needed a piece of equipment that cost $1,700, then that may also be reasonable for a larger employer but may not be for a smaller employer with less financial resources. The key is to remember that this analysis must be done on a case-by-case basis, and the outcome could be different for one location, site, or facility as compared to another location, site, or facility of the same employer.

2009 Changes: Q-and-A

Q: But what if an individual can use medication or a remedial device such as a prosthetic limb, known as mitigating measures, such that the individual is no longer disabled while using that medication or device; is the individual still covered under the ADA?
A: The answer is "Yes." This was one of several points of clarification in the new law. Mitigating measures other than ordinary eyeglasses or contact lenses shall not be considered in assessing whether an individual has a disability.

Q: What if an individual has a physical condition that is in remission and is currently experiencing no symptoms or adverse reactions; is this individual covered under the ADA?
A: Again, the answer is "Yes." The new law clarifies that an impairment that is episodic or in remission is a disability if it would substantially limit a major life activity when active.

Q: What does it mean to be regarded as disabled? Does it mean the individual has to be perceived to have a disability or that the individual must be perceived to have a disability that substantially limits one or more major life activities?

A: The answer is the former. The new law changes the definition of "regarded as" so that it no longer requires a showing that the employer perceived the individual to be substantially limited in a major life activity. Instead it provides that an individual is "regarded as" disabled if he is subject to an action prohibited by the ADA (e.g., failure to hire or termination) based on an impairment whether or not the impairment limits or is perceived to limit a major life activity.

Q: Does an employee who is regarded as disabled have the right to a reasonable accommodation?

A: No. This point was previously unclear, and federal circuit courts were issuing different decisions on this question. Under the new law, individuals who are covered only under the "regarded as" prong (they do not have an actual nor a record of a disability) are not entitled to reasonable accommodation. They are protected, however, under the anti-discrimination provisions of the ADA.

Suffice it to say that you should consult with your HR administrator or legal counsel if and when an employee tells you that he is having trouble successfully performing his job because of a physical or mental condition.

Family and Medical Leave Act

The federal Family and Medical Leave Act (FMLA) regulations were modified effective January 16, 2009, following a two-year public notice and comment period. The law still provides up to 12 workweeks of job protected leave in a 12-month period to an eligible employee and still generally applies to employers with 50 or more employees. An employer may still choose any 12-month period it prefers such as calendar year, fiscal year, or backward- or forward-rolling year (a separate 12-month period is specifically defined, however, for military caregiver leave, see below). An eligible employee continues to retain the right to be reinstated to the job he had upon returning from FMLA leave within the 12-week period. The following is intended to provide only a high-level overview of just some of the key aspects of the FMLA as it is administered today.

Which Employers Are Covered Under the FMLA?[4]

As mentioned above, employers that employ 50 or more employees are generally FMLA-covered employers. Coverage, however, does not apply on the very first day that an employer hires its 50th employee nor does coverage end of the same day an employer should fall below the 50-employee threshold. Let's say an FMLA-covered employer implemented a reduction in force 30 days ago. The employer now employs only 40 employees. Today an employee asks for FMLA leave. Is the employer an FMLA-covered employer today since it no longer employs at least 50 employees? It depends. It is important to remember that the definition of a covered employer is one that employs 50 or more employees for each working day during each of 20 or more calendar workweeks in the current or preceding calendar year. If, in the example above, the employer implemented its reduction in force (RIF) on June 1, then it would still be an FMLA-covered employer in this calendar year *and* the next calendar year (the 20th week of each year generally falls in May). On the flip side, if today an employer hires its 50th employee, it will not be an FMLA-covered employer until it has met the definition described above.

Which Employees Are Eligible for FMLA Leave?[5]

Eligible employees are still those that have worked for your company for a total of 12 months. Those 12 months need not be consecutive but must have occurred within the last seven years with some exceptions, such as absences for covered military service. For example, if an employee works for you for seven full months in this calendar year, resigns, and returns five years later and works for you for five full months, then that employee would have met the length-of-service requirements. In addition, however, the eligible employee must have also worked for your company for at least 1,250 hours within the immediately preceding 12 months. So, in the example above, the requirement for hours worked may not yet have been met (assuming full-time employment for five months, the employee might have worked only 21 weeks for 840 hours). But if the employee had worked for two full months initially and has now, five years later, worked for you for the last 10 full months on a full-time basis, then he probably has met the hours-of-service requirement. The eligible employee must also meet a third requirement: he must work at a site that employs at least 50 employees at or within 75 miles of that site. For example, let's say a financial institution has 125 employees. Forty employees work at the main office and the rest work at branches scattered throughout the state. If no branch, including the corporate office, is located within 75 miles of any other branch and no branch employs at least 50 employees, is any employee eligible for FMLA? No. While the financial institution may be an FMLA-covered employer, no employee is eligible because none works at a location that employs at least 50 employees at or within 75 miles.

For What Reasons May an Eligible Employee Take FMLA Leave?[6]

Leave is still provided for

(1) the birth and care of the newborn child of an employee;

(2) placement with the employee of a child for adoption or foster care;

(3) the care of an immediate family member (spouse, child under the age of 18 or otherwise incapable of self care, or parent) with a serious health condition; or

(4) taking medical leave when the employee is unable to work because of his own serious health condition.

In addition, there are new military leave provisions.

Military Caregiver Leave.[7] FMLA protections are now provided for employees who need to provide care for a family member who is a covered service member of the armed forces, including a member of the National Guard or Reserves, or a member of the armed forces, the National Guard, or Reserves who is on the temporary disability retired list, who has a serious injury or illness incurred in the line of duty on active duty for which he is undergoing medical treatment, recuperation, or therapy; or otherwise in outpatient status; or otherwise on the temporary disability retired list. For purposes of this leave, a family member includes spouse, son or daughter (of any age), or parent, or next of kin of a covered service member. Eligible employees are able to take up to 26 workweeks of leave in a 12-month period, inclusive of FMLA leave taken for other qualifying reasons. This 12-month period is specifically defined as starting from the first day leave is taken to care for a covered service member, so an employer may have to run two FMLA "clocks" for one employee: the 12-month period it has chosen for other types of FMLA leave (fiscal, calendar, backward-rolling) and this 12-month period.

Leave for Qualifying Exigencies for Families of National Guard and Reserves. Eligible employees may also take FMLA for certain qualifying exigencies to help manage the affairs of family members who are members of the National Guard and Reserves and who are on active duty. Qualifying exigencies are defined as:

(1) short-notice deployment;

(2) military events and related activities;

(3) childcare and school activities;

(4) financial and legal arrangements;

(5) counseling;

(6) rest and recuperation;

(7) post-deployment activities; and

(8) additional activities where the employer and employee agree to the leave.

For purposes of this type of leave, family member is defined as spouse, son or daughter (of any age), or parent.

Some other common questions and points of clarification include:

What Notice Must an Employer Provide to an Employee, and When and What Is the Penalty for Failing to Do So?[8] A covered employer must now provide an employee with the "Notice of Eligibility and Rights"[9] within five days from the time the employer learns of the employee's need for FMLA leave; previously, notice was required within two days. If an employee suffers individual harm because the employer did not follow the notification rules and provided the notice more than five days later, the employer may be liable for damages. (See Practical Tips at the end of this chapter; your managers are often critical in this part of the process.)

There is a new form that must also be provided to employees. In addition to the first "Notice of Eligibility and Rights," the employer must next provide the employee with a "Designation Notice."[10] While it is a new form that is required in addition to the myriad other forms and may add to the employer's administrative burden, it is intended to reduce misunderstandings. Under the former regulations, an employee would be given the FMLA "Response to Request" and medical certification form. The employee would then have his doctor complete the latter and return both, completed, to the employer. What happened next was sometimes anyone's guess. The employee would be absent and there was no documentation between the employer and employee to indicate whether the employer had received the documentation or was counting the absence as FMLA or not. The new Designation notice provides this express notice and documentation so both the employer and employee know, even if they do not agree, whether the leave is being designated as FMLA leave. This raises a common question: "What if an employee tells me that he does not want his qualifying leave to be counted as FMLA leave?" Under the FMLA, the employer retains the right to designate qualifying leave as FMLA. If the employer does not, then the employee may retain the right to a full 12 workweeks of FMLA leave, despite having already taken time off from work that qualifies for FMLA leave.

What Notice Must an Employee Provide to His Employer? Where an employee's need for FMLA leave is foreseeable, which is not the case in most instances in my experience, then the employee must provide the employer with at least 30 days of notice.[11] If the employee's need for leave is not foreseeable within 30 days, then the employee is required to give his employer notice as soon as is practicable.[12] An employer may require an employee to comply with the employer's usual and customary notice and procedural requirements for requesting leave, absent unusual circumstances. For example, if an employer has a policy that an employee must call his supervisor regarding any absence, then the employee taking FMLA leave may be required to do the same; e.g., telling a coworker to tell his supervisor that he will be absent may not be acceptable.

May an Employee Waive His FMLA Rights?[13] Yes, but only retrospectively. An employee may voluntarily settle an FMLA claim without prior approval of a court or the federal Department of Labor (DOL). However, prospective waivers of FMLA rights continue to be prohibited. For example, let's say you are giving an employee a severance agreement. The agreement includes, in exchange for salary continuation, a waiver of a long list of legal rights and claims (basically the employee promises to not sue the employer in exchange for the severance pay and benefits). The employer may properly include FMLA rights in the waiver but only with regard to any claims that may arise as of the date the employee signs the agreement; an employee may not properly waive his right to any future FMLA claims.

What Is the Definition of a Serious Health Condition?[14] The current regulations still define a serious health condition as one that involves either inpatient care or continuing treatment by a health care provider. Let's walk through a couple of examples.

If an employee is absent from work for three consecutive days and does not see a doctor, does that qualify for FMLA leave? Possibly not. The absence must be for more than three consecutive days or of a shorter period of time but intermittent and as a result of the same chronic health condition and, in either case, must include treatment by a health care provider.

So what if the employee is out for four consecutive days and calls his doctor, who puts him on a regimen of aspirin? Does that qualify as FMLA leave? Possibly not. The employee must have at least one in-person visit with the health care provider in order for the leave to qualify as FMLA leave and that visit must take place within seven days of the first day of incapacity. Generally, a regimen that includes over-the-counter medications such as aspirin, antihistamines, or salves, or bed-rest, drinking fluids, exercise, and other similar activities that can be initiated without a visit to a health care provider, is not, by itself, sufficient to constitute a regimen of continuing treatment for purposes of FMLA leave.

If the employee is never out for more than three consecutive days but is intermittently absent for a day or two here and there, does that qualify for FMLA leave? In the case of intermittent absences for a chronic health condition like asthma or migraine headaches, the absences must also include periodic visits (defined as at least twice a year) for treatment by a health care provider, or by a nurse under direct supervision of a health care provider.

Does "Light Duty" Work Count Towards FMLA?[15] No. Prior to the new regulations, at least two courts had held that the time an employee spent working in a light-duty position did count towards the use of FMLA leave, but that is no longer the case. Under the current regulations, time an employee spends working in a "light duty" position does not count against an employee's FMLA leave entitlement. But, this is balanced with a provision that the employee's right to reinstatement ends in the FMLA year used by the employer. So let's assume an employer uses the backward-rolling calendar year for FMLA purposes, which is what I find most employers use. An employee goes out on FMLA leave on June 1, but the employee is released to work light-duty eight weeks later. You have a light-duty position available and the employee accepts your offer, but the physician indicates that the duration of the need for light-duty is unknown at this time. Does the employer have to permit the employee to work in that light-duty position for more than the four remaining weeks of FMLA leave? Yes, because the time spent working in the light-duty position does not count against the employee's FMLA leave entitlement. So does the employer have to permit the employee to continue working in that light-duty position forever? No, the employee's right to be reinstated to his job expires on May 31 of the following year, which is the end of the FMLA year that his employer uses.

Does an Employee Who Is Absent on FMLA Leave Still Have the Right to Bonuses and Awards, Like a Perfect Attendance Award?[16] Not necessarily. The final rule changed how bonuses and awards like perfect attendance are treated. Today, an employer may deny a bonus or perfect attendance award to an employee who took FMLA leave — but only if the employer treats employees taking non-FMLA leave in an identical way. The perfect attendance example is pretty easy: as long as only those employees who incurred zero absences receive the award, then the employee who was absent under FMLA may be denied the award. But what about bonuses? What if an employer offers a pay-for-performance bonus program and an employee fails to meet a sales or productivity standard because he was absent on FMLA? Can the employee be denied this bonus? The answer is the same: yes, so long as other employees who missed the standard, regardless of the reason, are also denied the bonus. If a bonus or other payment is based on the achievement of a specified goal, such as hours worked, products sold, or perfect attendance, and the employee has not met the goal due to FMLA leave, then the payment may be denied, unless otherwise paid to employees on an equivalent leave status for a reason that does not qualify as FMLA leave.

May an Employer Contact an Employee's Physician to Get More Information? The final rule, which is the result of significant stakeholder feedback (including a September 2007 meeting at the DOL on "medical certifications"), recognizes the advent of the Health Insurance Portability and Accountability Act (or HIPAA) and the applicability of HIPAA's medical privacy rule to communications between employers and employees' health care providers. Responding to concerns about medical privacy, the rule adds a requirement that limits who may contact the health care provider and bans an employee's direct supervisor from making the contact. Here are two common scenarios:

First, you receive an employee's medical certification form and part of it is unclear to you. It's not unclear in the sense that you cannot read it, but you need clarification. Take the case of a medical certification that indicates, "The employee will need to rest periodically throughout the day." What does that mean? How many times per day will he need to rest and for how long each time? For what duration will this limitation last? In this instance, the employer must first give the employee an opportunity to provide more complete information within seven days. If the employee is unable or unwilling, then the employer is permitted to contact the employee's physician directly and simply ask for "clarification." The employer is to *not* request any additional medical information but to simply ask for clarification of the information already provided.

The second scenario is similar but different from the example above. This time let's say the medical certification form is clear and you understand it, but it appears that it may not be valid. Perhaps it is completed in two different colors of ink, in two different handwriting styles, or perhaps there are some smudges or cross-outs and it appears that some information was changed. You want the employee's physician to authenticate the form; that is, you want the employee's physician to confirm that he did, in fact, complete the entire form as you see it. In this instance, the same rule as described above applies.

In either instance, for clarification or authentication, the question arises as to who may contact the employee's physician.[17] To make such contact, the employer must use a health care provider, an HR professional, a leave administrator, or a management official. Under no circumstances, however, may the employee's direct supervisor contact the employee's health care provider.

Military Leave

The Uniformed Services Employment and Reemployment Rights Act (USERRA) is a federal law that provides certain employment protections to individuals called to serve in the uniformed services, including active and inactive training. The DOL offers online training programs to introduce employers to the rules and regulations surrounding USERRA.[18] There are two issues I see commonly arise and of which employers should be aware. First, there are the reinstatement rights of persons returning from covered service. Most employers seem to know that covered individuals generally have the right to be reinstated to their job for up to five years (with eight exceptions). Some employers, however, are not aware of the "escalator clause." Unlike FMLA, which requires reinstatement to the job the employee had when he went out on leave, USERRA provides that the covered employee shall be reinstated to the job he would have had had the employee not gone out on covered military leave. That means the employee should be reinstated to the position he had when he left plus any promotions, pay increases, enhanced benefits, etc., that the employee would reasonably have been expected to receive had the employee not gone out on leave.

The second matter is related to continued employment. In chapter 6, we talk about at-will employment, and even if you have not yet read that chapter, I suspect you know what that is. Employment at-will simply means that the employment relationship continues only at the will of both parties; either party may terminate the employment relationship at any time, for any reason, with or without notice. But when an employee returns from covered service of more than 30 days, that employee is no longer an at-will employee for either six months or one year, depending upon how long the employee served in the uniformed services. The employee may not be discharged except for cause. For example, let's say a company has a reduction in force (RIF) policy that is based on seniority; e.g., the last hired are the first laid off (LIFO — last in, first out). A company is experiencing serious financial difficulties and finds that it must implement a RIF. In accordance with its policy, it plans to abolish the positions of the last 10 people hired, one of whom is an employee who was reinstated three months ago after returning from covered service. Can the employer RIF this employee? The answer is "No." The company must go to the 11th person on the list.

You should also check the laws in your states of operation; many have laws that provide certain rights and protections for individuals called to service in the state militia.

Court Appearances—Jury/Witness Leave

There are currently no federal laws that require employers to give leave to individuals called to appear in court; many states do have such laws, however. I find the more common right is related to jury service. Some state laws provide that an employee's absence to serve on a jury may not be the sole reason for adverse action, such as issuing corrective action or terminating employment; others provide that an employee may not be subject to any adverse employment action for such service, whether it is the sole reason or not. Yet others expand that protection to include those who are victims of a crime or are summoned as a witness. Some require that the time off be paid, others do not.

Voting Leave

As of this writing there is also currently no federal law that requires employers to provide leave for individuals to vote. At least 23 states, however, require employers to provide employees with time off from work to vote,[19] and some states qualify that time off must be granted only if the employee is not already scheduled time off from work for some minimum period of time such as one to two hours while the polls are open. Some states require employers to provide time off from work to vote and that the time off must be paid.

Parental Leave

Other than the FMLA, as of this writing there is no federal law that requires employers to provide time off for parental leave. As of this writing, however, there is federal legislation pending that could do so. Work-life balance has been a "hot" topic for several years now and is getting national attention. On May 18, 2009 (the first work day after Mother's Day), federal legislation (Healthy Families Act) was introduced to require employers with 15 or more employees to provide at least one hour of paid leave for every 30 hours worked to a maximum of 56 hours per year. Accrual would start on the first day of employment and could be used by the employee not later than the 60th day. Leave would have to carry over from year to year and may be used for the employee's own illness or to care for a relative or for victims of domestic violence. There are also several other, similar pieces of legislation pending. If you are an HR professional reading this book, membership in SHRM and/or an affiliated, local chapter in your state can provide you with regular legislative updates so you can monitor federal and state legislation. You might also check to see if your company belongs to a local or state chamber of commerce. These, too, are often great resources for tracking legislation, particularly at the local level. Another trend has been efforts at the federal level to amend Title VII of the Civil Rights Act to prohibit discrimination in employment based on parental status. Once again, many states have laws that do provide certain leave, paid or unpaid, for employees who need to take time off from work for a variety of related reasons, such as to care for an immediate family member, to attend a child's school-related activity, and more.

Practical Tips

- *Train your management team members.* They do not have to know all the details or ins-and-outs of the FMLA, ADA, and the myriad other leave laws. But they are generally on the front line and are the first to know if an employee has a qualifying absence or condition. Too often we hear stories of an HR administrator who hears for the first time from a supervisor that an employee has been absent from work for several weeks. At that point, the employer may have already failed to provide the FMLA notice in a timely manner (within five days). It can be a proactive practice to train managers regarding some initial "bells and whistles" that can alert them as to when they should contact human resources or the company's leave administrator.

- *Policy development.*
  › Whether you use the DOL's sample policy or have created your own, be sure to define the year in which your employees may take up to 12 workweeks of leave; e.g., calendar, fiscal or backward rolling. Many employers use the latter as it is most advan-

tageous to the employer. The federal regulations provide that where an employer fails to select a specific 12-month period, the option that provides the most beneficial outcome for the employee will be used.[20] For example, let's say you intended to use the backward-rolling year but your policy was silent. An employee then uses 12 weeks of FMLA leave from October through December. On January 1, the employee requests an additional 12 weeks of leave. While you might reply that the employee had exhausted all 12 weeks and will not be eligible again until October of the current year, the employee might say, in accordance with the federal regulations, that since your policy was silent the employee is eligible for another 12 weeks with the start of the new calendar year, effectively giving the employee 24 weeks of job-protected leave in a six-month period.

> Review your EEO and harassment policies. If they do not already include disability — as well as other legally protected categories such as race, religion, gender, and national origin — consider adding it. If your policies do not already include prohibiting discrimination and harassment on the basis of a person's perceived disability as well as their association with a person with a disability, consider adding those as well.

> Clearly address employee eligibility by including the reference to working at a site that employs 50 or more employees at or within 75 miles. If you do not do so, then employees working at smaller sites may read the policy, request FMLA leave and then become quite frustrated or disappointed when told they are not eligible. If that happens, you may have not just an employee relations issue on your hands but a court may hold that your policy created an express or implied contract and, absent the clarifying term to the definition of eligibility, you may be obligated to grant FMLA leave to that employee.

• If your company has employment practices liability insurance (EPLI), then check with your carrier to determine if they will give your company a discount if it has a specific ADA policy in the employee handbook and/or conducts an HR compliance audit. If your company does not carry EPLI coverage, then you may want to contact several insurance carriers to get several quotes to compare.

- Consider joining a professional or trade association (you or your company) such as SHRM, a chamber of commerce, or an industry-specific trade or professional organization that can help you stay abreast of changing laws and regulations, particularly if your company is a multi-state employer.

- Know your state laws. Again, many states have laws that require employers to provide a certain amount of leave, paid or unpaid, to employees for family, medical, military, voting, and other reasons. Be sure your policies comply with federal and state law requirements.

Maintaining an Inclusive Workplace

People, Perception, and Communication

How often have you had an employee come to you and say that someone was getting on the employee's nerves? The employee proceeds to tell you what this other person does or says and why the employee thinks it is rude or unfair, using all sorts of not-so-flattering adjectives and labels to describe the person. And when you finally ask that employee, "Well, what did that person say when you told him what you are telling me now?" what answer do you get? The employee tells you that he has not said anything; he wants you to fix it. And that is your job, in part. You are the complaint department, whether you are a front-line supervisor, manager, director, or HR administrator. Your role is to foster, facilitate, and maintain positive employee relations. I mentioned at the start of chapter 3 that you should take complaints as a compliment. An employee will not complain to you if he does not trust you.

But effective workplace communication is a shared responsibility. So encourage the employee to find a way he might approach this coworker and appropriately share his concerns. Communication is critical to maintaining positive employee relations and is a responsibility that should be shared by every employee in your organization.

Many years ago I came across the concept of the "Johari Window." You may have heard of this. When I read about it, I was so struck by how on point it was and how it could be so practically applied to everyday life that I have incorporated it into harassment training programs ever since.

The Johari Window is a cognitive psychological tool created by Joseph Luft and Harry Ingham in 1955, used to help people better understand their interpersonal communication and relationships.[1] Figure 5.1 is my modified version but it very closely mirrors the actual model.

Figure 5.1	
The self that **I KNOW**	The self that **I PORTRAY FOR OTHERS**
The self that **I BELIEVE OTHERS PERCEIVE**	The self that **OTHERS ACTUALLY PERCEIVE**

The upper left pane of the window, the "self that I know," is exclusive to me. For example, have you ever had something bad or sad happen in your personal life? And when you come to work the next day someone with the very best of intentions comes up to you and says, "I'm so sorry to hear what happened, I know exactly how you feel." What is likely your first reaction? You may think, "No you don't." You may appreciate the sentiment and the person's effort to empathize. Although the same thing may have happened to that person, the loss of a loved one, family separation, etc., how they reacted to that is likely not exactly the same as your reaction.

The upper right pane of the window, the "self that I portray for others," changes constantly throughout the day and is driven primarily by the person and the context or situation. How I present myself varies depending upon with whom I am communicating at the moment: a close friend, my boss, a client, a stranger, etc. It is also dependent upon the situation, where I am: work, happy hour, or a holiday gathering of family and friends. Thus, I try to present a particular image or make a particular impression depending upon the person to whom I am speaking and the situation or context of the conversation.

The lower left pane of the window, the "self that I believe others perceive," is a result of my personal observation of others. Let's say I am giving a public presentation, as I often do, and I see someone in the audience roll his eyes. My first thought is likely that the eye-roll is in response to something I just said and that person strongly disagrees with me and thinks what I said is wrong or stupid. Now I am thinking about how to overcome that reaction and re-establish credibility with that member of my audience.

That brings us to the lower right pane of the window, the "self that others actually perceive." Take my audience member described above. It may be, in fact, that his eye-roll had nothing to do with anything I said. He just realized that he forgot to turn off the coffee maker at his house that morning and is worried because he can't remember if the coffee maker has an automatic shut-off or not.

So what happens? Without communication our perceptions change our behavior. I start modifying my presentation style because I am worried about the audience member I perceive to be dissatisfied, now I go off track and my audience is wondering where I am going and why.

At a more practical level, this happens so frequently when employee relations go awry. Person "A" says something in a group and person "B" is offended. Person "B" does not say anything but the next time "A" says "Hello," "B" does not respond. Now "A" is wondering what "B's" problem is and the two slowly stop communicating and the problems grow from there.

The more you can encourage employees to talk to one another the less likely it is that workplace miscommunications will occur. For me, miscommunication often is the seed that later blossoms into unlawful workplace harassment. How many times has an employee told you that he is being harassed? And when you ask for more detail what you hear is not a form of unlawful harassment but one of perception about what someone else said or did that may or may not be what that person intended. Here's another example: Have you ever gone to an alleged harasser to explain the nature of a complaint and after explaining what the person allegedly said or did that offended someone, the person becomes very angry? The person asks why the individual did not just say something to him instead of going to the manager or human resources, protesting, "I'm not a mind reader!" Or the person becomes very apologetic, proclaiming, "Oh my gosh, I'm so sorry. I didn't mean it that way!" The bottom line: open communication can prevent myriad problems.

So with that as our foundation you recognize that it is your role to encourage open and appropriate dialogue between employees. It is also your responsibility, whether you are a manager, supervisor, or HR professional, to monitor the workplace, maintain positive employee relations, and prevent and correct unlawful harassment.

So what *is* unlawful workplace harassment and what are the current trends?

First, I assume that anyone reading this book has most likely taken some type of harassment training somewhere in their career. As a result, this chapter assumes you know the basics of unlawful harassment, particularly sexual harassment, so we won't cover that. What we will cover are some of the latest trends, tips, tools, and reminders for proactive practices.

What *Is* Unlawful Harassment?

Remember that there is a wide range of unkind, uncivil, inappropriate, and unprofessional behavior that is not unlawful harassment. It is, however, more likely than not that such behavior is a violation of your company's policy or code of conduct. To constitute unlawful harassment, remember that the behavior complained of must be based on a person's membership in a legally protected class. This may also include if an individual is perceived to be a member of a legally protected class, or if the person is discriminated against, or harassment based upon his association with a person in a legally protected class. For example, let's say an employee reports that his supervisor is harassing him. When asked to explain what is happening, the employee describes close and constant supervision, being counseled every time he is just a few minutes late for work, and being constantly reminded about performance errors. Is this descriptive of unlawful harassment? Not based on the description above. It sounds like the employee is not performing satisfactorily, and, while he may feel harassed, it is not unlawful. What is missing to constitute unlawful harassment? Some indication that the manager is treating this employee differently from other employees who are similarly situated and that difference in treatment is based on the employee's membership in a protected class. Try the next scenario.

Now let's spin that fact pattern: Now the employee describes his harassment the same as above and adds that he is aware of female coworkers who also come in late, have an error rate equal to or greater than his, but who are not constantly and closely supervised or counseled. Could this constitute unlawful harassment or some form of discrimination? It could. What we hear in this description is at least a perceived difference in treatment that may be based on the employee's membership in a protected class; i.e., his gender.

Keep Yourself (and Your Company) Safe

Courts are not unanimous in their interpretation of whether an individual manager or supervisor may be held liable under Title VII of the Civil Rights Act for unlawful harassment or discrimination. So to be safe, presume you can be. And, because you may be given certain power and authority by the company to run business operations, including directing the work of employees, it is also likely that you are acting as an agent of the employer and can create legal liability not only for yourself but for the company by what you say or do (or fail to do). Your actions and your knowledge, and what you see, hear and know, may be implied to be actions or knowledge of the company. So if you see or hear something that could be a violation of the law, you should tell your HR representative or, if you are the HR representative, begin an investigation.

Remember, too, that investigations can be very informal processes. An investigation is just a process by which you try to get to the truth of the matter. For example, an employee comes into your office and says he heard from Coworker A that Coworker B is feeling harassed by the courier who delivers mail each day. How do you investigate? It may be as simple as going to Coworker B and asking if everything is "OK" and if there is anything or anyone in the work environment, including any third party, who is making him uncomfortable. What is likely the first question Coworker B will ask you? "Who told you that?!" Must you disclose your source? No. You may simply tell Coworker B that is not important and remind him that you do not know this for a fact. It was just brought to your attention as a possibility and you wanted to check and understand what was happening and ensure everything is "OK." This can also be a great opportunity to remind the employee about your company's anti-harassment policy, the no-retaliation provision, and what resources he may use to report any concerns he may have.

In addition to statutes like Title VII, individual managers and HR professionals may face liability under a variety of tort claims. These are claims such as defamation, assault and battery, false imprisonment, intentional infliction of emotional distress, and invasion of privacy that are filed between or against individuals. Below are a few examples. The theme here is to help keep yourself, and your company, safe (or at least reduce the potential for legal liability).

Defamation — a manager berates an employee in the hallway in front of some of the employee's coworkers, yelling that the employee is an "incompetent waste of company resources." Based on this description alone, does it sound as though this employee was just subjected to unlawful harassment? Probably not; there is nothing in the description that indicates the behavior was directed at the employee because of his membership in a legally protected class. But what other legal claim might be available to this employee? I guess the heading above gave this one away — defamation. What defense might the employer have? The truth; I may not defame you if I tell the truth about you. So what evidence does this company now have to provide in light of the manager's ranting? The company would have to show that the employee is, in fact, an incompetent waste of company resources. Even if the company could produce that evidence, at what cost after all the time and attorney's fees? See the section below on workplace bullying; while it may not constitute unlawful harassment, such conduct can create legal liability for the bully as well as the company that employs him.

It is also important, I think, to mention workplace gossip here as well. Not only is gossip generally inappropriate and unprofessional, it can severely damage relationships between coworkers. Rumors about what people are (not) doing in their personal lives, with others, coworkers, clients, customers, vendors, or others should be promptly addressed and stopped. You want to encourage employees to share any concerns about behaviors that impact working relationships or that violate your company policy, such as a no fraternization rule, to human resources or a manager but not to peers, coworkers, or colleagues. Rumors of extramarital affairs, for example, can lead to claims of defamation or slander between coworkers, not to mention damage good working relationships among coworkers. It can be a proactive practice to incorporate a bit about this potential personal liability in your harassment prevention training programs so employees understand that gossip is not only contrary to your company policy or philosophy but could also land them in legal turmoil.

Assault & Battery, False Imprisonment, and Intentional Infliction of Emotional Distress — Here we can illustrate all three issues in one story. A manager calls an employee into his office to provide some coaching regarding unsatisfactory work performance. The employee comes in and sits across from the manager, who is seated at his desk, which faces the window, so the employee has his back to the window and is facing the office door. The manager is seated behind the desk between the employee and the office door. During the coaching session the employee becomes irritated, stands, and shouts, "I don't have to put up with this!" and begins to walk around the manager's desk towards the office door. Simultaneously, the manager stands, steps to the side of the desk towards the employee (are you getting the picture?) and touches the employee's elbow saying, "Wait, don't go." The employee subsequently files a lawsuit citing: (1) assault and battery from the touching of his elbow; (2) false imprisonment from when the manager stood he was between the employee and the office door, blocking the employee's way out of the office; and (3) intentional infliction of emotional distress — the employee alleges that the manager was intentionally abusive and now the employee has such distress that he is having trouble eating, sleeping, etc., and is under a doctor's care.

Lessons learned? Don't touch your employees! How productive will the meeting be at this point anyway? As the employee begins to leave your office you retain control by telling the employee he needs to return in 5 or 10 minutes after he has had a chance to compose himself. Keep yourself safe. Unfortunately and sadly, violence is an issue in today's workplace. Don't switch places and let the employee sit between you and the office door. Consider placing chairs in an office that are equidistant to the door so that if either you or the employee feels the need to step out of the room either of you can do so comfortably.

Invasion of Privacy — This is an issue with which I think employers struggle, perhaps more than either of the others described above. How do you balance the humanitarian desire to support and comfort an employee who has experienced a death in the family or critical diagnosis without breaching privacy (not to mention violating the Health Insurance Portability and Accountability Act or HIPAA)? Here's an example. There is a small department and everyone knows each other well and has worked together for years. Several employees come to the manager one day and ask if everything is "OK" because one of their coworkers has been absent for over a week. They are genuinely concerned. The manager expresses his appreciation for their concern and proceeds to reassure them that everything will be fine and discloses that the employee (female) recently had a mastectomy. The manager reassures the employees that the prognosis for a full recovery is very good and the employee is expected to return to work in a few weeks. The employees decide to pool their money and send their coworker flowers and a get well card. Is the employee happy when she receives this sentiment from her coworkers? No. She sues for invasion of privacy and wins. Lessons learned? Do not disclose personal, not to mention medical, information about employees to other employees or coworkers. As a manager, you may have a business need to disclose certain information to human resources or vice versa but not to the employee's coworkers. You might say something like, "I appreciate your concern and I am sure this employee would too. However, just as I would respect your privacy and not disclose personal information about you to a coworker, I need to respect this person's privacy and do the same here. I will certainly let the employee know that you asked about him."

Workplace Bullying

In August 2007, the Workplace Bullying Institute (WBI) published results from a survey completed by nearly 8,000 people and conducted by WBI and Zogby International.[2] Follow-up surveys were conducted in 2010.[3]

The surveys defined bullying as, "sabotage that prevents work from getting done, verbal abuse, threatening conduct, intimidation, humiliation, or exploitation of a known vulnerability (psychological or physical)." Here are some of the results from the 2007 survey that you may find of interest (visit the websites listed in the endnotes to download a free, full copy of the survey results).

- 37 percent of the respondents indicated that they are (13 percent) or have been (24 percent) a victim of workplace bullying;

- 40 percent of those who felt that they were or had been bullied never reported it to their employer;

- 40 percent of those who felt they were or had been bullied quit their job because of the bullying; and

- Bullying is four times more prevalent than unlawful harassment (e.g., only one out of every five claims of bullying involves some form of unlawful harassment).

If you extrapolate this data to your own workplace, then roughly one out of every three employees feels he is or has been a victim of workplace bullying, many will not tell you about it, and just as many may leave your organization because of it. This is just another example of why open communication is critical to maintaining positive employee relations.

Practical Tips

- When an employee tells you that he is being harassed, ask the employee to describe the behaviors or actions that are occurring. If they are being directed at the employee, ask the employee why he thinks he is the target of the behavior. Then listen. If the employee replies that he thinks it is because of his membership in a legally protected class such as the employee's age, race, religion, gender, nationality, disability, etc., consider it a report of unlawful harassment and then begin an investigation. If you do not hear any reference to membership in a protected class, do not ignore it; this could still signal an employee relations matter and you should take steps to facilitate and resolve the matter.

- I shared this tip in the previous chapter and feel compelled to do so again here. If your company has employment practices liability insurance (EPLI), check with your carrier to determine if it will give your company a discount if you have conducted or will conduct regular, periodic harassment training, have specific anti-harassment policies in your company's employee handbook, and/or conduct an HR compliance audit. If your company does not carry EPLI coverage, you may want to contact several insurance carriers to get several quotes to compare.

- You can save time and money by providing combined training programs with managers and staff together, rather than having separate training programs for each. An advantage is that in the core program, everyone will hear the same message at the same time. If you do so, it would then also be wise to provide at least a 30-minute supplemental training program immediately following the core program for your management team members only. Use this time to tell them a bit about their duty to prevent and correct unlawful harassment, their duties as an agent of the employer, and a few words about individual and corporate liability.

6

What's in a Name? Properly Classifying Your Workers

We classify our workers in a number of ways. First, we consider whether the worker is an employee or if the person falls under some other type of working relationship (volunteer, unpaid intern, independent contractor). Once we determine that the worker is an employee, we need to determine whether the employee qualifies for exempt status or must be classified as non-exempt. In addition, what will be the nature of the employment relationship? Will it be at-will, contractual, a combination of the two (as they are not necessarily mutually exclusive), or something else? This chapter addresses some key concepts in each of these areas.

Plenty of people perform work for your company. But not every worker is necessarily an employee. You may have vendors, independent contractors, contractors, subcontractors, agency temps, leased workers from a professional employer organization (PEO), volunteers, interns, and more. So let's consider some of these.

Independent Contractors

The headlines are replete with news of lawsuits and litigation in which an employer is found to have improperly classified a worker or workers as an independent contractor (IC) instead of an employee. I had the distinct honor of testifying before a congressional joint subcommittee hearing on behalf of SHRM on the challenges employers face when trying to make the proper determination as to the proper classification of a worker as an employee or independent contractor. There are just too many definitions of employee and independent contractor! From federal statutes to agency guidance from the Internal Revenue Service (IRS) to state laws including workers' compensation and unemployment insurance, they all vary. I have seen it happen more than once where an employer follows the IRS guidance. When the project is finished and the work is completed, the IC then files for unemployment insurance (UI). Despite the employer having followed the IRS guidance, the state agency disagrees with the classification because the agency uses a different test. The agency then holds the employer liable for back UI taxes. In some cases, the employer is also held liable for back wages if the worker(s) should have been classified as a non-exempt employee and worked overtime. States are also enacting legislation that makes the misclassification of a worker as an IC instead of an employee illegal subject to fines and penalties and, in some instances, jail time. As of this writing, at least 20 states have passed laws, issued an executive order, or considered legislation addressing the improper classification of employees as independent contractors.[1]

So where do you begin to assess the nature of the employment relationship? Many of you reading this may be familiar with the IRS 20-factor test or 1099 rule, which has generally been replaced with a three-factor test that includes at least seven sub-factors.[2] The three key factors are behavioral control, financial control, and relationship of the parties. Consider the following guidance from the IRS:

- If you give your worker extensive instructions on how work is to be done, then this suggests that the worker is an employee.

- If you provide the worker with training about required procedures and methods, then this suggests that the worker may be an employee.

- If the worker has invested a significant amount of money into his work, then he may be an independent contractor. While there is no precise dollar test, the investment must have substance. However, a significant investment is not necessary to be an independent contractor.

- If you do not reimburse the worker for some or all of his business expenses, then the worker may be an independent contractor, especially if his unreimbursed business expenses are high.

- If the worker can realize a profit or incur a loss, this suggests that he is in business for himself and is an independent contractor.

- If you provide the worker with benefits, such as insurance, pension, or paid leave, then this is an indication that the worker is an employee.

- A written contract may show what both you and the worker intend. This may be very significant if it is difficult, if not impossible, to determine status based on other facts.

While clearly there is no one rule or method that is foolproof, you should keep in mind that control is a key issue. Certainly you have to tell a worker what to do and define or establish the parameters that must be met with regard to quality, timeliness, etc. When you start exerting direction or control, however, over the "manner and means" by which the worker gets the job done, you start down a slippery slope. The manner and means include telling the worker where, when, and how the worker must do the *what*. Misclassifying workers can have adverse consequences for your company related to workers' compensation coverage, ERISA liability, union organizing drives, Family and Medical Leave Act (FMLA) coverage, tax liability, and more. So consider this IRS guidance as well as any applicable definitions in the laws or regulations in your state(s) of business operation(s).

Interns and Volunteers

Each spring many employers contemplate having interns — usually students, retired persons, or displaced workers seeking to remain active in the workforce — perform work for them during the summer months, holidays, or seasonal periods when the volume of business increases. A common question is if and when these individuals must be paid and how much. Unpaid internships are permitted under the Fair Labor Standards Act (FLSA)[3] and employers should ensure that their intern(s) meet all of the following factors:

1. The internship, even though it includes actual operation of the facilities of the employer, is similar to training which would be given in an educational environment;

2. The internship experience is for the benefit of the intern;

3. The intern does not displace regular employees, but works under close supervision of existing staff;

4. The employer that provides the training derives no immediate advantage from the activities of the intern; and, on occasion, its operations may actually be impeded;

5. The intern is not necessarily entitled to a job at the conclusion of the internship; and

6. The employer and the intern understand that the intern is not entitled to wages for the time spent in the internship.

If any one factor is not met, it may indicate that the person cannot be properly classified as an unpaid intern. For example, let's say your company recently had a reduction in force (RIF) and placed a temporary freeze on hiring any new employees. Simultaneously, you have a lot going on; your company is changing its payroll system and HRIS system, and you are also a government contractor and it is time for you to update your written affirmative action plans. With so much on your plate, you do not have time to get these tasks done but you cannot hire someone to help you, even on a part-time, temporary basis. So you think about contacting a local college to find an intern to do this work for free. Would these assignments qualify for an unpaid internship? Apply the questions above, particularly question three. While the intern may work under close supervision, is he not actually displacing another worker? You are seeking an intern because you cannot hire. If you did not have the hiring freeze, you might actually hire a temporary, part-time employee to do this work. If that is the case, then you may not meet all elements to properly use this intern with no pay. On the other hand, if your company is providing job shadowing opportunities that allow an intern to learn certain functions under the close and constant supervision of regular employees, but the intern performs no or minimal work, the activity is more likely to be viewed as a bona fide education experience. So what is the remedy? In this scenario, there may not be one since there is a hiring freeze. In another instance, the company could simply bring the student intern on and pay him minimum wage (of course the higher of federal or state) for the time worked. The federal Department of Labor (DOL) also notes that unpaid internships in the public sector and for non-profit charitable organizations, where the intern volunteers without expectation of compensation, are generally permissible.

And what about volunteers? As the economy changes, many people seek new ways of networking to find employment opportunities: Young workers may be drawn to volunteer roles to gain practical work experience that may lead to employment; and older workers who have retired may volunteer their time to business so they may continue to serve the local business community. Whatever the individual's motivation, the employer needs to ensure that these individuals properly qualify for unpaid volunteer status. The DOL provides that volunteers are usually:

•   Working part time;

•   For public service, religious, or humanitarian objectives; and

•   For religious, charitable, and similar nonprofit corporations.

This test may be less strict than the one for interns. Where the latter requires that all six elements or factors be met, a volunteer could work full-time but it is less likely. Thus, a volunteer who sits with babies in the neo-natal intensive care unit of a local hospital, who volunteers his time to walk dogs at the local animal shelter, or who volunteers at a local soup kitchen, may qualify for volunteer status. The FLSA makes a special exception under certain circumstances for individuals who volunteer to perform services for a state or local government agency and for individuals who volunteer for humanitarian purposes. When an individual performs work, however, that does not meet all of the above factors, the employer might be wise to classify the worker as a part-time employee and pay at least minimum wage.

The Basic Nature of the Employment Relationship

Now that you have determined that a worker is, in fact, your employee, what will define the nature of that employment relationship?

At-Will Employment

Currently, 49 of our 50 states are at-will employment states. Generally, employment at-will means the employment relationship will only continue at the will of both parties; that is, employment may be terminated by either party (the employee or employer), at any time, for any reason or no reason, with or without notice. As of this writing, Montana is the exception and has a law that permits employers only to discharge an employee for "good cause," except during the employer's probationary period. If the employer does not define a probationary period, then that period is presumed to be six months.[4] The nature of the at-will employment relationship, however, does not permit an employer to take adverse employment action (discharge, demotion, corrective action, etc.) for unlawful reasons. The latter could include action based upon an employee's actual or perceived membership in a legally protected class such as age, race, religion, gender, nationality, disability, etc. The same may apply to the status of an individual with whom an employee associates. Chapter 3 helps explain why an employer should take the time to groom its employees despite the fact that the employment relationship continues only at the will of both parties.

Contractual Employment

Some employers use employment contracts for certain newly hired employees; some may use them for executives; some may use them for sales staff that incorporate a non-compete and/or no-solicitation agreement; and some may use them to simply spell out the expectations of the relationship. Contractual employment does not have to be mutually exclusive of at-will employment. It is very possible to have a contract with one of your employees that also clarifies that the employment relationship is at-will and can be terminated by either party at any time.

Collective Bargaining Agreements

These create another type of relationship that is not at-will. Collective bargaining agreements (CBAs) commonly provide that members of the union may not be terminated from employment without "just cause." That is, the employer must provide a reason for the termination, such as excessive absenteeism, lateness, poor work performance, etc. The CBA may then spell out what steps the employer must take before taking any adverse action and what rights the employee has upon receipt of such action, such as filing a grievance or compelling arbitration. If you started this book from the beginning, which is the end of the employment relationship, you read the pre-termination checklist. Those considerations are actually regularly used by arbitrators in the collective bargaining arena, known as the elements of just cause. While I have found that those elements vary in number and description from author to author, the five elements I have described in chapter 1 are those I have found to be generally common. That is why I find them to be a great, proactive guide when considering terminating the employment of any employee, union or non-union.

FLSA Status

A step that may be subsequent to determining the nature of the employment relationship is assessing whether the employee qualifies for exempt status under the FLSA. A proactive and conservative approach is to operate from the presumption that every employee is non-exempt; that is, the employee must be paid on an hourly basis, earn at least minimum wage (federal or state, whichever is higher), and one and one-half times the employee's regular rate of pay for each hour worked over 40 in any workweek. You, the employer, have the burden to show that any employee qualifies for exempt classification. In order to establish that qualification, you must bear the burden of proof and demonstrate that three key elements or "tests" under the federal regulations have been met. The employee must: (1) be paid a guaranteed minimum salary of at least $455 per week; (2) be paid on a salary basis; *and* (3) meet one of three duties tests.

Executive, Professional, or Administrative

The DOL has published online video presentations that explain each classification and fact sheets that provide more detail.[5] Remember that the individual must meet all three tests: guaranteed minimum salary, salary basis, and duties. If the employee is not paid at least $455 per week, then you need go no further in the analysis. If the individual is paid at least $455 per week but is not paid on a salary basis because you deduct for quality or quantity, then you need go no further in the analysis; the person cannot qualify for exempt status. And if the person is paid the minimum, guaranteed salary, but does not meet at least one of the duties tests, then he must be classified as non-exempt. Here is a high-level overview of each test:

Minimum Salary Test

The individual must generally be paid a guaranteed minimum salary of at least $455 per week with a few exceptions such as for teachers, attorneys, and physicians.[6] In the case of computer professional employees, the compensation requirement also may be met by compensation on an hourly basis at a rate not less than $27.63 an hour. The salary may not be prorated for part-time employees. The employer may, however, provide additional compensation over and above the guaranteed minimum salary. Let's say a tax firm wants to offer its certified public accountants a bonus for all the additional hours they are working during tax season; a hospital wants to pay an incentive bonus to registered nurses who volunteer to work extra shifts; or a firm wants to give its management team members a bonus at the close of a positive fiscal year. These may all be permissible.

Salary Basis Test

The individual must be paid a guaranteed minimum salary that is not subject to reduction because of variations in the quality or quantity of the work performed.[7] There are seven exceptions to this rule under the federal regulations:

1. Deductions from pay may be made when an exempt employee is absent from work for one or more full days for personal reasons, other than sickness or disability. Thus, if an employee is absent for two full days to handle personal affairs, the employee's salaried status will not be affected if deductions are made from the salary for two full-day absences. However, if an exempt employee is absent for one-and-a-half days for personal reasons, the employer can deduct only for the one full-day absence.

2. Deductions from pay may be made for absences of one or more full days occasioned by sickness or disability (including work-related accidents) if the deduction is made in accordance with a bona fide plan, policy, or practice of providing compensation for loss of salary occasioned by such sickness or disability. The employer is not required to pay any portion of the employee's salary for full-day absences for which the employee receives compensation under the plan, policy, or practice. Deductions for such full-day absences also may be made before the employee has qualified under the plan, policy, or practice, and after the employee has exhausted the leave allowance in accordance with such plan, policy, or practice. Thus, for example, if an employer maintains a short-term disability insurance plan providing salary replacement for 12 weeks starting on

the fourth day of absence, the employer may make deductions from pay for the three days of absence before the employee qualifies for benefits under the plan; for the 12 weeks in which the employee receives salary replacement benefits under the plan; and for absences after the employee has exhausted the 12 weeks of salary replacement benefits. Similarly, an employer may make deductions from pay for absences of one or more full days if salary replacement benefits are provided under a state disability insurance law or under a state workers' compensation law.

3. While an employer cannot make deductions from pay for absences of an exempt employee occasioned by jury duty, attendance as a witness, or temporary military leave, the employer can offset any amounts received by an employee as jury fees, witness fees, or military pay for a particular week against the salary due for that particular week without loss of the exemption.

4. Deductions from pay of exempt employees may be made for penalties imposed in good faith for infractions of safety rules of major significance. Safety rules of major significance include those relating to the prevention of serious danger in the workplace or to other employees, such as rules prohibiting smoking in explosive plants, oil refineries, and coal mines.

5. Deductions from pay of exempt employees may be made for unpaid disciplinary suspensions of one or more full days imposed in good faith for infractions of workplace conduct rules. Such suspensions must be imposed pursuant to a written policy applicable to all employees. Thus, for example, an employer may suspend an exempt employee without pay for three days for violating a generally applicable written policy prohibiting sexual harassment. Similarly, an employer may suspend an exempt employee without pay for 12 days for violating a generally applicable written policy prohibiting workplace violence.

6. An employer is not required to pay the full salary in the initial or terminal week of employment. Rather, an employer may pay a

proportionate part of an employee's full salary for the time actually worked in the first and last week of employment. In such weeks, the payment of an hourly or daily equivalent of the employee's full salary for the time actually worked will meet the requirement. However, employees are not paid on a salary basis within the meaning of these regulations if they are employed occasionally for a few days, and the employer pays them a proportionate part of the weekly salary when so employed.

7. An employer is not required to pay the full salary for weeks in which an exempt employee takes unpaid leave under the FMLA. Rather, when an exempt employee takes unpaid leave under the FMLA, an employer may pay a proportionate part of the full salary for time actually worked. For example, if an employee who normally works 40 hours per week uses four hours of unpaid leave under the FMLA, the employer could deduct 10 percent of the employee's normal salary that week.

Each winter, questions also arise as to whether an employer may require exempt employees to use paid leave and/or make deductions from exempt employees' wages for full or partial day absences due to inclement weather. The DOL has issued a number of opinion letters on this matter.[8] The general answer is that employers may require an exempt employee to use paid leave for such absences. If the exempt employee has exhausted all paid leave, then the employer may deduct from the exempt employee's wage for a full day absence but not a partial day of absence.

Another common question is with regard to making deductions from an exempt employee's wages for lost or damaged company property. For example, let's say a company issues an identification badge to all employees. The company has a policy that if an employee loses or damages his ID badge, a $10 fee will be deducted from the employee's wage to replace the badge. According to a DOL opinion letter, that policy defeats the salary basis of payment for an exempt employee.[9] What if the employer did not deduct the replacement fee from the exempt employee's wage but required him to pay the fee directly to the employer? The DOL opinion letter indicates that is effectively the same as a deduction and would also violate the salary basis of payment.

Duties Tests: Executive, Professional, and Administrative Exemption

Executive Exemption

In January 2009, the DOL reported, "The violation cited in the greatest number of cases was one in which the employees did not meet the duties test required for exempt executive employees. Violations of the executive duties test were cited in 524 cases and resulted in back wages of $3.4 million for approximately 2,600 employees. Although cited in fewer cases, back wages resulting from determinations that employees failed to meet the duties test for administratively exempt employees were nearly $4 million and affected approximately 2,900 employees."[10] Industries with the greatest number of cases were restaurants, followed by agriculture followed by health care. In order for an employee to qualify for exempt status under the executive exemption, he must meet each of the following tests:

- The employee's primary duty must be managing the enterprise, or managing a customarily recognized department or subdivision of the enterprise;

- The employee must customarily and regularly direct the work of at least two or more other full-time employees or their equivalent; and

- The employee must have the authority to hire or fire other employees, or the employee's suggestions and recommendations as to the hiring, firing, advancement, promotion, or any other change of status of other employees must be given particular weight.[11]

Employers often get tripped up in this category when a team leader, supervisor, or manager performs both exempt and non-exempt duties.

A supervisor who has the authority to hire and fire, and regularly supervises two or more full-time equivalents (FTEs), but who also performs non-exempt duties, must perform those non-exempt duties on average less than 50 percent for his regular work hours to be properly classified as exempt.

Administrative Exemption

In order to qualify for exempt status under the administrative exemption, an employee must meet each of the following tests:

- The employee's primary duty must be the performance of office or non-manual work directly related to the management or general business operations of the employer or the employer's customers; and

- The employee's primary duty includes the exercise of discretion and independent judgment with respect to matters of significance.[12]

This title can be misleading. You may read the title "Administrative" and think that it refers to administrative assistants (AA). While an AA may be properly classified as exempt, this exemption refers to an individual who administers business operations such as developing and implementing marketing plans and programs, developing and administering human resource policies, and engaging in contract negotiations with vendors and contractors as just a few examples. Having the authority to independently exercise control over these activities is a critical component to qualifying for this exemption.

Professional Exemption

In order to qualify for exempt status under the professional exemption, an employee must meet each of the following tests:

- The employee's primary duty must be the performance of work requiring advanced knowledge, defined as work which is predominantly intellectual in character and which includes work requiring the consistent exercise of discretion and judgment;

- The advanced knowledge must be in a field of science or learning; and

- The advanced knowledge must be customarily acquired by a prolonged course of specialized intellectual instruction.

A key here is to remember that the job requires the advanced degree and not just that the individual has the advanced degree. For example, if a librarian has a master's in library science degree but the job he holds does not *require* that degree, then he may not qualify for the professional exemption. The employee may, however, qualify for exempt status under the executive or administrative exemption.

Remember that the above analyses must be conducted for each employee, not just by job classification. For example, you might have five incumbents in the same job classification who all meet the duties test and are paid on a salary basis. But if one is a part-time employee and earns less than $455 per week, that individual would have to be classified as non-exempt. Or perhaps all five are paid on a salary basis and meet the minimum salary test but one is a sub-par performer and, while the job requires the exercise of discretion and independent judgment, this one employee is not fulfilling those duties. That employee may have to be classified as non-exempt.

As of this writing there are at least 17 states that have their own wage and hour regulations that define these exempt classifications differently from the federal regulations.[13] If you have business operations in any of these states, then you will need to conduct a dual analysis and repeat this process following the regulations in your state(s). Also be sure that any wage deductions you make are also in accordance with the wage and hour laws of the state(s) in which you do business. Many states have laws that prohibit certain deductions that are otherwise permissible under federal law.

Practical Tips

- Just because employment is at-will does not mean you have no liability when terminating the employment relationship. Let bona fide business needs, not emotion, drive your employment decisions.

- When in doubt, classify conservatively:

  › If you conduct an FLSA analysis and are still not sure whether a position fully qualifies for exempt status, then classify the position as non-exempt.

  › If you conduct a classification analysis and are still not sure whether a worker will be an employee or independent contractor, then classify the worker as an employee.

- If you use unpaid, student interns, or volunteers, be sure they meet the "tests" described in this chapter. If not, or if you are unsure, then classify them as employees and pay them at least minimum wage.

- Be sure the terms of any employment contract provide you with the flexibility you want or need and do not obligate you to terms or conditions of employment that you did not intend.

7

Employee Handbooks:
Read 'Em and Weep?

Like performance appraisals, all too often an employee handbook is used by a plaintiff to demonstrate or establish that his employer created an implied or express contract or created some obligation it did not otherwise intend. This chapter is intended only as a general guide for some proactive practices to consider when creating or updating your company's employee handbook. Remember to always consult with your company's legal counsel to ensure your policies, practices, and procedures comply with the federal, state, and local laws and regulations in your states of operation.

A common first question is, "*Should we have an employee handbook?*" or "*Must we have an employee handbook?*" Under federal law, there is no requirement that an employer have an employee handbook. It is up to you. There are, however, advantages and disadvantages of having one. Advantages include:

1. Introducing employees to your company, its goals, mission, and expectations; use the handbook as an opportunity to brag about your company and share its history;

2. Providing clarification for your employees as to their benefits and your expectations; and

3. Helping to ensure consistency in providing benefits like paid leave, when you will/not provide training opportunities, promote from within or provide coaching, counseling, and correcting.

Disadvantages of employee handbooks generally arise only when they are not drafted well. Examples may include when an employer unintentionally creates an implied contract or defeats the at-will employment relationship. We will consider some examples later in this chapter.

A next common question is, *"What should we include in our employee handbook?"* A challenge in creating a useful employee handbook is creating one that provides your employees with enough information to know what is expected of them and what they can expect from your company while not including so much information that the handbook becomes so large that no one will read it. You also want to avoid including so much detail that you lose some of your discretion in making management decisions. At the end of this chapter, I have enclosed a sample table of contents as a general guide for some policies that seem to be common among many employers (see figure 7.1 at the end of the chapter). Some, of course, may not be applicable to your company, such as FMLA requirements that generally do not apply to employers with less than 50 employees. You should have an employment attorney review your employee handbook, whether it is your first or an updated version, to ensure it is compliant with the federal, state, and local laws and regulations that are applicable to your company. There are companies and vendors that offer or sell template employee handbooks, as well as employment applications. That is fine and certainly can save you a lot of up front work. It is likely, however, that the template will need to be tailored to not just meet your company's procedures, policies, and practices but to also comply with the laws and regulations of your state(s) and local jurisdictions.

So now that we have answered two common, threshold questions, let's address some proactive practices and pitfalls to avoid for some of the more common policies.

EEO & Anti-Harassment Policy Tips

Most if not all employee handbooks have equal employment opportunity (EEO) and anti-harassment policies. That's great, but what is important is what a proactive EEO policy actually includes. Most list a number of protected classes and might read, "We do not tolerate any form of unlawful discrimination and provide equal employment opportunities without regard to an individual's age, race, religion, color, sex, national origin, or disability." That statement covers key protected classes covered under federal law, but not all, such as citizenship, genetic information, or military status. And there may be additional protected classes under your state or local laws. Since these protections change through the legislative process and would require you to rewrite your handbook every time a new federal, state, or local law is passed, you might include a caveat at the end of the sentence that reads, "... or on any other legally protected basis under federal, state, or local law." That lets the reader know that you know you have not listed all protected classes.

It may also be a proactive practice to include perception and association clauses in your EEO policy. Remember that Title VII of the Civil Rights Act of 1964 as well as the Americans with Disabilities Act (ADA) prohibit discrimination, which includes unlawful harassment based on the perception of an individual's membership in a protected class as well as the legally protected status of an individual with whom the employee associates.

What about your harassment policy? In 1999, the Equal Employment Opportunity Commission (EEOC) published guidance on what elements it recommends an employer include in a proactive harassment policy.

An anti-harassment policy and complaint procedure should contain, at a minimum, the following elements:

- A clear explanation of prohibited conduct;

- Assurance that employees who make complaints of harassment or provide information related to such complaints will be protected against retaliation;

- A clearly described complaint process that provides accessible avenues of complaint;

- Assurance that the employer will protect the confidentiality of harassment complaints to the extent possible;

- A complaint process that provides a prompt, thorough, and impartial investigation; and

- Assurance that the employer will take immediate and appropriate corrective action when it determines that harassment has occurred.[1]

Employment Status Policy Tips

With some frequency, employee handbooks refer to full- and part-time employees but do not define these. In this case, an employee working anything less than 40 hours may be unsure if he is full- or part-time, such as if the employee works 35 hours per week. When defining full- and part-time, be sure to not leave a gap. For example, a policy might define full-time as being regularly scheduled to work at least 40 hours per week and part-time as scheduled to work less than 35 hours per week. In this example, employees regularly scheduled to work at least 35 but less than 40 hours may be unclear as to whether they are full- or part-time employees.

Another proactive practice may be to use the term "regular" rather than "permanent" employees. The very nature of the at-will employment relationship, as well as many contractual employment relationships, is that employment is *not* permanent or guaranteed for any particular length of time or duration.

Now, remember the reference at the start of this chapter about how employee handbooks can create an unintended but enforceable implied contract? The probationary or introductory period policy is a great example. You may read in this type of policy that this period is "a time to put your best foot forward" and that the employer can let the employee go during this period, with or without notice or reason. So if you are a new employee and just read that policy, what might you think it implies? What impression do you have? Does it sound like something magical happens at the end of that introductory period? Does it sound like the employer might not be able to terminate you with or without notice or reason after this period? If you answered "Yes," some courts would agree.

Some courts have held that this type of language may create an implied contract because of the implication as described above. So should you have an introductory period policy? Ask yourself this, "Why do you want one?" How is the employment relationship during this period different from the day after this period? If there is no difference, then you probably do not want or need this policy. But if, for example, you do not permit employees in this period to accrue paid leave, or perhaps they can accrue it but cannot use it, then use this policy to describe those differences.

Pay Issue Policy Tips

Many state laws require employers to give employees notice of their pay rate and day upon hire. You may be able to meet this requirement by including that information in your employee handbook. Many pay issues are regulated by state laws and are too numerous to address here. A few pay issues that are commonly regulated at the state level include and are not limited to:

- *Pay at termination of wages and accrued, paid leave.* Some state laws require the payment of accrued paid leave under certain circumstances. And some state laws require you to issue the final paycheck within a certain period of time, depending upon whether the employee quit or was involuntarily terminated.

- *Pay frequency.* Some states require that employees, at least non-exempt, be paid at some interval more frequently than monthly, such as at least twice per month.

- *Payday that falls on a holiday or non-work day.* Some states require that if the payday falls on a holiday or other day that the employer is not open for business, then employees must be paid the immediately preceding holiday. For example, a policy that provides that if the payday falls on a Sunday, then employees will be paid on Monday would not be permissible. Some states require that the employees would have to be paid on Friday.

- *Direct deposit.* Some states limit or restrict an employer from requiring direct deposit.

- *Deductions from pay.* Some states prohibit certain deductions that may otherwise be permissible under the Fair Labor Standards Act (FLSA) such as for cash shortages, lost or damaged company property, negative paid leave bank balances, and more.

Common to most all employers is the requirement under the FLSA that overtime be paid to non-exempt employees for all hours worked over 40 in a workweek. Keep in mind that your policy should read (and the law requires) that overtime is 1.5 times the employee's regular rate of pay, which may be different from the employee's hourly rate of pay. It may be proactive to use the phrase "regular" rate rather than "hourly" in your related policies. For example, if a non-exempt employee's hourly rate of pay is $10.00 and he receives a non-discretionary bonus of $100.00 for exceeding a particular performance or productivity goal in a one-month period, the value of the bonus may have to be calculated into the employee's hourly rate of pay for all hours worked in that month to determine his regular rate of pay for overtime calculations.

In addition, consider including the "safe harbor" policy provided by the Department of Labor (DOL) from the 2004 regulations. If an employer has a clearly communicated policy that prohibits improper pay deductions and includes a complaint mechanism, reimburses employees for any improper deductions, and makes a good faith commitment to comply in the future, such employer will not lose the exemption for any employees unless the employer willfully violates the policy by continuing to make improper deductions after receiving employee complaints. The best evidence of a clearly communicated policy is a written policy that was distributed to employees prior to the improper pay deductions by, for example, providing a copy of the policy to employees at the time of hire, publishing the policy in an employee handbook, or publishing the policy on the employer's Intranet.[2]

Why reinvent the wheel? The DOL has provided a sample "salary basis" policy that employers can use to incorporate into the company's employee handbook or related pay policies.[3]

Paid and Unpaid Leave

Aside from Family and Medical Leave Act (FMLA) leave for covered employers, there are myriad other forms of leave that employers may offer. Some are paid; some are not. We discussed the administrative considerations and some policy tips in the chapter 4. Aside from those, many employers offer some type of "personal" leave that may include time off for personal reasons or medical reasons that are not covered under FMLA. Once again, check the employment laws and regulations in your state(s) of operation to ensure these policies comply with any state requirements. For example, some states may require certain employers to offer such leave, some may require that such leave be accompanied with pay, and some may require that such leave be available for the employee to care for an immediate family member as well as for the employee's own illness.

In addition, consider the following:

- Does your policy address whether "personal" leave is in addition to or runs concurrent with any other type of leave that you offer, such as paid leave?

- Does your policy let employees know whether they may or are required to exhaust any paid leave (vacation, sick, paid time off or PTO) before being absent without pay?

- Does your policy include a maximum length of time that you may approve such an unpaid leave of absence, such as six months or the employee's length of employment, whichever is less?

- Does your policy indicate for how long the employer will continue the employee on medical coverage, such as for 30 days or until the end of the month in which paid leave is exhausted?

- Does your policy include a notice indicating whether or not you will guarantee an employee reinstatement to the same position he had when he began the leave and, if not, what considerations you will offer, such as any comparable position for which he qualifies or any position for which he qualifies?

- If you expect employees on leave to not apply for unemployment insurance benefits, does your policy expressly provide a notice to that effect, and what may happen if the employee does file for unemployment insurance (UI) benefits?

Professional Appearance

Dress code policies have received a fair amount of attention over the last few years, as they may violate Title VII. An employer's policy that strictly prohibits things like visible tattoos, piercings, and certain clothing may violate an employee's right to religious accommodation under Title VII. There have been cases addressing an employer's strict dress code and whether it violates Title VII as a result of an employee's religious observance. Here are a few examples.

Body Piercing

Sylvia has several tattoos and has recently had her nose and eyebrows pierced. A newly hired manager implements a dress code that requires that employees have no visible piercings or tattoos. Sylvia says that her tattoos and piercings are religious because they reflect her belief in body art as self-expression and should be accommodated. However, the evidence demonstrates that her tattoos and piercings are not related to any religious belief system. For example, they do not function as a symbol of any religious belief, and do not relate to any "ultimate concerns" such as life, purpose, death, humanity's place in the universe, or right and wrong, and they are not part of a moral or ethical belief system. Therefore, her belief is a personal preference that is not religious in nature. But if this employee's piercings were a part of a sincerely held religious belief then the employer may be required to provide a religious accommodation, such as offering some options such as wearing no jewelry in the piercings during work hours or wearing a clear, plastic insert instead of jewelry.[4]

Visible Tattoos

In this case, a court found the employer failed to offer an employee a religious accommodation for his Kemetic religion, an ancient Egyptian faith. As a part of his practice, the employee received religious inscriptions in the form of tattoos. The inscriptions, less than a quarter-inch wide and encircling his wrists, are a verse from an Egyptian scripture and are written in a liturgical Egyptian language. The inscriptions symbolized his dedication and servitude to his creator, and the employee's belief made it a sin to intentionally conceal the religious inscriptions. The employee had the inscriptions on his wrists when he was hired by the employer, which had a dress code that prohibited employees from having visible tattoos. The Equal Employment Opportunity Commission (EEOC) said that although the employee had worked for the employer for six months without complaint from customers, coworkers or his immediate supervisor, a new manager saw the tattoos and fired the employee for not concealing them. The employee filed a lawsuit, which was settled for $150,000.[5]

Facial Hair and Hair Styles

In one case, the EEOC filed a lawsuit asserting an employer engaged in unlawful religious discrimination when it refused to hire a Rastafarian as a driver helper because he wore a beard. The employee contended that his beard was part of his observance of Rastafarianism. The employer then offered him an "inside" job only, one that would not have contact with the public. EEOC guidance also indicates that "no-beard" policies may also discriminate based on race against African-American men who have a predisposition to *pseudofolliculitis barbae* (severe shaving bumps) unless the policy is job related and consistent with business necessity. In yet another case, the EEOC filed a lawsuit on behalf of a Muslim employee who was allegedly denied a workplace accommodation for her sincerely held Islamic religious beliefs and practices when she sought permission to cover her head with a scarf during the holy month of Ramadan and her employer denied her request.[6]

Policies that separately itemize what constitutes acceptable attire for men as compared to women may also give rise to a claim of gender discrimination. A critical component in developing a dress code is to focus on your business needs. Where certain attire is prohibited ask, "Why?" If it poses a safety hazard, then the restriction may be appropriate. For example, a hospital might properly implement a policy that its direct-care providers may wear only post or clip-on earrings but no hoop earrings to reduce the likelihood of injury in the event a patient becomes combative and tries to pull the dangling earring from an employee's ear.

Next, be willing to consider providing an accommodation in these situations. For example, security officers may be prohibited from having hair beyond a certain length. The rationale may be a safety issue and, like the example above, be intended to prevent a combative individual from grabbing and pulling the officer's hair. In this case, if an applicant or employee indicated that cutting his hair would violate a tenet of his faith, the employer might require the individual to securely tie his hair back while at work. The EEOC has also issued guidance for employers on dress code and related policies and practices.[7]

Electronic Communications

Technology seems to be in a race with itself advancing faster all the time. Just a few years ago, employers' key concerns were related to e-mail and Internet use. Now it is all about social networking and whether or how much to limit (if at all) employees' use of blogs and other social networking sites on and off company time and property. The rules here are particularly different for public- (government) versus private-sector employers because of the constitutional implications related to freedom of speech for public-sector employers. As with the dress code, let your business needs drive your employment practices. Why and when do you want to restrict employees' use of these systems? Prohibiting use during paid working time may be to reap the full return on the investment of your wages; you are paying employees to work, not visit chat rooms or blogs. When you begin to regulate what employees do off company time and property, the matter becomes grayer. What about the employee who uses a company issued laptop during non-working hours to publish his dissatisfaction with the company on a personal webpage? Then taking it one step further, what about the employee who does the same but uses his own computer on his own time? For these issues, as with all, you should consult with your company's legal counsel for guidance on what you may and may not properly restrict, how, and when.

Practical Tips

- *Policy versus Practice*. Remember that no matter how well your employee handbook is written, it is only as good as you apply and enforce it. If you rarely enforce any particular policy, the day you want to do so may likely be the day you give the appearance of adverse treatment based on an individual's protected status.

- *Consistency*. As has been mentioned throughout this book, this does not mean that you have to treat every employee in exactly the same way. You may make exceptions to the rule and treat employees equitably rather than equally. Be sure, however, you have a valid business reason for making an exception.

- Sometimes it might be better to have no employee handbook than an old or outdated one. There is no strict rule, but consider updating your handbook at least every 12 to 18 months. You will likely find that even if federal employment laws have not changed, there may be new federal or state regulations, new state or local laws, or case law that has modified the interpretations of existing laws.

Figure 7.1 | [COMPANY NAME] EMPLOYEE HANDBOOK

TABLE OF CONTENTS--SAMPLE	Page
INTRODUCTION (About the Company)	
Disclaimer	
EQUAL EMPLOYMENT OPPORTUNITY	
UNLAWFUL HARASSMENT	
EMPLOYMENT STATUS HOURS AND PAY	
Attendance	
Direct Deposit	
Employee Status & Classification	
Expense Reimbursement	
Inclement Weather	
Introductory Period	
Overtime	
Pay Periods and Days	
Performance Appraisals	
Promotion/Transfer	
Reduction in Force	
Time Sheets/Records	
Work Week	
Day and Hours	
PAID AND UNPAID LEAVE [can sort categories into headers with Paid and Unpaid Leave]	
FMLA	
Funeral/Bereavement	
Holidays	
Jury Duty	
Military Leave of Absence	
Personal Leave of Absence	
Sick Leave	
Vacation	
EMPLOYEE BENEFITS AND SERVICES	
Continuation of Benefits (COBRA or small employer)	
Employee Assistance Program (EAP)	
Flexible Spending Account (FSA)	
Health (can include dental and vision)	
Parking	
Pension (401(k), 403(b), SIMPLE IRA etc.)	
Tuition Reimbursement	

continued on next page

Figure 7.1 | [COMPANY NAME] EMPLOYEE HANDBOOK

TABLE OF CONTENTS--SAMPLE	Page
Workers' Compensation Insurance	
WORKPLACE POLICIES AND STANDARDS OF CONDUCT	
Appearance — Work Area	
Bulletin Boards	
Cell Phones	
Change of Information	
Communication Policy	
Company Property	
Confidentiality	
Conflict of Interest	
Courtesy	
Disclosure of Employee Information	
Emergency Procedures	
Employee Conduct	
Gifts and Gratuities Policy	
Hiring of Relatives	
Open Door Policy	
Outside Employment	
Professional Appearance	
Safety	
Searches	
Smoking Policy	
Solicitation and Distribution of Literature	
Substance Abuse Policy	
Telephone Use	
Use of Company Name	
Visitors	
Voice-Mail and E-Mail Policy	
Workplace Violence Prevention	
CORRECTIVE ACTION AND SEPARATION FROM EMPLOYMENT	

8

Welcome Onboard

It is your employee's first day of work and you have already invested a lot of time and money to get him there, right? You advertised, reviewed resumes, interviewed candidates, and perhaps conducted some pre-employment assessments or post-offer medical exams or questionnaires. Now how do you begin to reap a reward and positive return on the investment (ROI) on all that time and money? Onboarding is a term that has come into its own over the last several years. What is the difference between new employee orientation (NEO) and onboarding? Is the latter just a new name for what employers have done for years or is it truly different? The answer is, of course, it depends. You can give the program you have for new employees most any name. The question is what is it, what is it intended to do, and what does it actually do?

I distinguish between the two (NEO and onboarding) as an event versus a process. New employee orientation is an event; onboarding is a process. Neither is right or wrong, good or bad; they are, however, different. Onboarding provides employees with an ongoing process by which they are acclimated to your company's mission, vision, philosophy, methodologies, business operations, procedures, and more. It is broader in scope and more in depth.

I remember my second job out of undergraduate school was as an assistant branch manager at a bank. I was so impressed by the depth of its onboarding program (and this was in the 1980s!). Of course, the bank did not call it onboarding at the time. But it was a full, four-week program by which I was introduced to nearly every department in the bank, spending a half to a full day in each so I could understand the behind-the-scenes processes of how checks were collected and sent to the Federal Reserve, how mortgages were processed and approved or denied, what marketing did to reach corporate versus individual customers, how payroll worked, and more. When I got my first job in human resources in 1989, one of my first charges was to revamp the NEO program. While it was not expanded to the scope described above, it was expanded to include not only more information about the hospital's history and mission but to also to include different speakers, including members of the executive team to talk about our history, mission, and vision; a union representative to jointly present information about benefits (the rep would meet in a separate group with new employees who would be working in one of the bargaining units to talk about union membership); and our rabbi (this was a Jewish founded and funded institution) to talk about some of the basic tenets of the Jewish faith. The latter was borne out of two experiences. The first was my own experience as a new employee. We had two cafeterias, the main one and a smaller, kosher cafeteria. Not knowing better, one day I walked into the kosher cafeteria with a container of popcorn. As I entered the cafeteria there were shouts and people called to me. I was startled and did not understand until someone approached me and explained that non-kosher foods were not permitted inside and that was the purpose of a wooden board that had been attached to the wall just outside the door. It looked like a tray attached and set perpendicular to the wall so people could set their non-kosher food items on the tray before they entered the cafeteria. What an "Aha" moment!

The second was an instance in which a nursing technician was going to be issued corrective action for shouting at a patient. An elderly patient had repeatedly called out from her bed for assistance. The nursing tech came into the room and reminded the patient that she did not have to shout; she could simply press the electric call button that was next to her in the bed. A few minutes later the patient needed assistance and again called out loud. The nursing tech again reminded the patient to not shout but to press the call button. After another exchange or two the technician lost her patience and yelled at the patient telling her to stop disrupting others by calling out. It was later discovered that the patient was an Orthodox Jew and this event happened on a Friday evening, which was this patient's Sabbath. What the technician did not know, and what we failed to tell her as the employer, was that during this Sabbath an observant follower is not permitted to use electronic devices. So this patient could not use the call button; that was why she was shouting. Another "Aha" moment! So providing some information about the basic tenets of the Jewish faith only made sense to help our employees better serve our diverse patient, employee, and visitor population!

So where do you begin? The program that is best for your organization depends upon many factors: your company size; how many employees you hire each month or week; your industry; what is important to you that employees know and understand; and so much more. A full blown onboarding program may not be feasible for a smaller employer. But if you consider some of the basic elements, a modified version may be a great fit for most any employer.

Pre-Employment Engagement

Do you engage your newly hired employee before his first day of work? The Gallup Organization reports the following:

- "[O]rganizations that have optimized engagement have 2.6 times the earnings per share (EPS) growth rate compared to organizations with lower engagement in their same industry."

- In average organizations, the ratio of engaged to actively disengaged employees is 1.5:1.

- Within the U.S. workforce, Gallup estimates the cost of disengagement to be more than $300 billion in lost productivity alone.[1]

So how do you engage your employees from the moment they accept your offer? Some employers may invite the employee and immediate family members to visit the worksite, have a guided tour, meet the employee's new manager and HR representative to welcome them, and help them feel a part of the new "community." This, of course, takes time and may not be feasible in all industries, particularly if the worksite is a contracted or government worksite or an otherwise secured facility. You could tailor this process to one that will work for you, your organization, and the new employee.

Day One

If your company is smaller or hires just a few employees each month, then you may choose to orient new employees one-on-one rather than in a large group as part of a new employee orientation program. Larger employers may have monthly or semi-monthly NEO programs with 20 or more employees in the audience for each program. Whichever method you develop and use, be sure each employee's first day is interactive. The ideal is not to give the employee a copy of your employee handbook and that big, fat folder with all the new-hire paperwork and forms and have the employee sit at a desk all day reading through the material (I had this experience one time and was so disappointed and bored!). Engage the employee from Day One. Tours are great. No matter in which department the employee will work, provide a tour of all or at least some key departments and those that are appropriate (again safety, security or other considerations may preclude touring in some areas). The more the employee understands the scope of the entire organization's processes and not just those of his department the more apt the employee is to feel a part of the entire organization and understand how his work and the work of his department contributes to company-wide operations.

Ease the paperwork burden. Each of us has likely experienced the overwhelming volume of paper and information you receive the first day on the job, from benefits (life, health, pension/401(k), STD, LTD) to payroll (timesheets, direct deposit, tax forms) and so much more. It may be helpful to provide all the information on Day One and then to have a rolling review over the next several days by which you can come back to the employee and review key topics; e.g., Day Two — collect completed I-9 and payroll/tax forms and answer related questions; Day Three — collect completed health/welfare/pension forms and answer related questions, etc.

Another process and tool I found useful when I was in human resources was a departmental orientation checklist. Working in a hospital with more than 3,500 employees, our NEO program covered a high-level overview of our mission, vision, history, benefits, performance appraisal process, and more. What it could not address were specific departmental policies, standards, and expectations, which varied widely from clinical to non-clinical operations and even within and across non-clinical departments. The expectations we had for HR staff differed from those working in clinical areas, facilities, transportation, housekeeping, and more. Consider developing a departmental orientation checklist for each department to share and review with employees hired in a specific department. While the same checklist will likely be used by all managers working in the same department, the checklists may vary from department to department. Checklist items may include: dress code; attendance and punctuality; opening and closing procedures; equipment/machinery use and maintenance; meal and rest periods; shifts; and more. This may be more difficult than you think. There is so much we take for granted when we come to work. To develop a checklist for your department, consider talking to one or two of your newest employees. Ask them what questions they had in their first day, week, and month that could have been better addressed. You may decide you need to drill down one more level and develop a checklist for various jobs within certain departments as the expectations listed above may also vary within a department for employees working in different jobs.

Job Shadowing, Mentoring, and On-the-Job Training

Whether your onboarding program is one week or one month, you will want to establish a method or process by which the new employee has a key contact for day-to-day interaction, learning, and feedback. Some companies have a formal on-the-job-training (OJT) or job shadowing program by which high performers may volunteer and are selected to serve as mentors to new employees. The new employee may shadow the mentor for the first week or so to learn the specifics of the new job related to procedures and processes. As with the NEO process that implements a departmental orientation checklist, a checklist for OJT is helpful as well. This can help ensure consistency in the training of new employees in the same job classification. While the output or productivity of the new employee will likely be lower during this period, the cost of lower productivity may be well offset by the avoidance of or subsequent reduction in errors that may result from a more fully informed and trained employee.

Where job shadowing is not feasible, some employers may still provide a mentor. The mentor, again, may be a more senior and top-performing employee to whom the new employee can go to ask questions or seek clarification about job processes or procedures. This process is less formal and may likely not include a checklist but serves as a resource and key contact for the new employee to lend additional support during the initial learning curve.

Feedback

You can learn a lot about your onboarding process by including a formal process by which the supervisor of the new employee and the employee can provide feedback. The supervisor, using both the onboarding and departmental orientation checklists can ensure all areas, topics, and issues have been covered and can provide the new employee with feedback regarding his performance to date. Likewise, and just as important, the new employee can provide feedback to the company about the onboarding process. This can be done in a stop-start-continue format. That is, what should we stop including in our onboarding process because it did not work well or did not add value? What should we start including in our onboarding process that would add value? What should we continue to include in our onboarding process because it worked well? And, of course, asking the new employee for related feedback, such as: What portions of the onboarding process should we modify or fine tune to enhance the process?

A Few Words about Retention

You can do a fabulous job of welcoming, orientating, and/or onboarding your employees. But don't stop there. Retaining your top performers has myriad benefits to an employer and its employees. High retention means lower turnover, which may reduce time and costs related to recruitment, selection, hiring, and training. Top performers may also help enhance employee relations and morale by serving as mentors and role models for employees who are not yet performing as well as they can. So how do you figure out how to keep these employees? Ask them! Find out what keeps them with your organization.

Sometimes referred to as a "stay interview," this dialogue can range from informal one-to-one conversations, to facilitated group discussions, to web-based surveys. Trained managers, HR professionals, or third-party facilitators may seek feedback on what policies, practices, and procedures the company should stop, start and continue to enhance retention (much like the dialogue described in chapter 1 related to feedback). Some employers may not want to hear the responses, such as those to the question, "What should we stop doing?" But even if some of the responses are hard to hear, the feedback can be invaluable. You can't fix a problem if you don't know that it exists. Finding out what can be fine tuned now can save lots of time and money later.

At what point employers use this process will vary; some may conduct stay interviews periodically, such as annually as a proactive way of keeping their finger on the pulse of employee preferences. Others may implement stay interviews in advance of making a change such as implementing a new policy or practice like new flexible work arrangements or benefits. When and how you engage your top performers to get their feedback will depend upon what works best for your organization; just be sure you use the data and information you obtain. Don't let the survey results sit on a shelf!

Practical Tips

- *Collaborate.* A key to a successful onboarding program is collaborative development. Build your program with input from executive team members, department managers, front-line supervisors, human resources, and employees actually doing the work. You may be surprised what you will hear is important to each group. With this feedback, you can develop a well-rounded program that meets the needs of the entire organization, across all levels, and from a variety of perspectives.

- *Give the Big and Little Picture.* It can be helpful to provide the new employee with a copy of the company's organizational chart and departmental chart if the roles within the department are not spelled out on the organizational chart. This way, the employee can see where he fits into the organization and can lead to a discussion about succession planning, career ladders, and more.

Foreword: Practice Your Passion!

For those of you looking for information to professionally grow, learn, or advance, this Foreword is for you.

Are you happy in your job? I don't mean, "Yeah, it's OK," I mean are you really happy? Do you really enjoy what you do or do you do it because you have to pay the bills? One study conducted by the University of Chicago in 2007 found that less than half (48 percent) of people interviewed between 1972 and 2006 said they were very satisfied with their job.[1] Another found that over half were "very happy."[2] I suspect those numbers may vary as the economy and job security varies.

How about this: do you know what you want to be "when you grow up?" If you answered "No" to either of those questions, you clearly are not alone. It was probably not until about seven years ago, one year after I had started my own practice, that I could honestly and wholeheartedly answer "Yes" to both of those questions. I love my job and hope I never have to do anything else. Now others have asked me how I got here. So, with all humility, I am happy to share some thoughts with you in the hope that you might find the same contentment.

First, I would ask, did you find your job or did your job find you? I did not seek a role in human resources administration; it found me when I stumbled upon it. It was my junior year in undergraduate school and my parents and I agreed that I should find a summer job. We happened to find a summer intern program at the Social Security Administration. I applied and was accepted. The job happened to be in the HR department. I loved it! That stumble set me on a path that lead me to where I am today. Sure, there have been diversions. At the close of my summer internship it was pretty much agreed that I would return after I graduated and have a job. As fate would have it, however, that was the year President Reagan put a temporary freeze on federal hiring. So when I graduated the economy was slow and, after searching for a few months, I ended up taking a job as a teller in a credit union. That diversion lasted about six years in the banking and finance industry. But I never lost the HR bug.

It takes patience and diligence and it's not easy sometimes. I know many of you reading this book know that. I looked and looked, applied and applied for jobs in human resources, but was not hired because I had no experience. So I went back to school, took classes at night, and completed my Master's degree. Within about four months of getting my degree, I landed my first job in human resources. I was so excited. I was back on the path ... for awhile.

Sure, there have been other diversions along the way too. After spending nearly 10 years in HR administration, I was getting a little burnt out. I had also gone to law school at night, graduated, and had passed the bar exam. I did not want to litigate nor did I want to leave human resources and move into our corporate counsel's office. I also had a fabulous vice president of human resources whom I figured was not going to leave anytime soon (I reported directly to her) so I think this was the point at which I started wondering, "What do I want to do when I grow up?" So I ended up taking a job in academia and outside of human resources. As I transitioned to my new employer I was worried, nervous, and scared that I had made the wrong choice professionally. But you know what? That turned out OK too. After about two years I looked at my career path, where I had been, and where it looked like I was going, and decided I had veered off track; I was not where I wanted to be. But where did I want to be? I *still* did not know what I wanted to do when I "grew up!"

So I started networking. I began calling colleagues (consultants, attorneys, and HR executives) whom I respected and who were in places

I thought I might want to be. Those informal chats over coffee or lunch led to two job offers: one in human resources and one with a law firm. Believe it or not, I chose the latter. Once again, I left my HR path and diverged. But guess what? That worked out well, too. After about two years, the process repeated itself; I was not on a path I loved (although I knew I was getting close) and, once again, had to ask, "What *do* I want to do when I grow up?!"

Then, with lots of trepidation and even more support from my husband, then current employer, colleagues, clients, and friends, I took the plunge and fearfully but with excitement went out on my own. Today I am on a path that I am sure could be no better. I am happy and I love what I do. And the neatest part is that it was not planned. It was the result of some calculated stumbling.

So I share this with you not as a way of saying what is or is not the right way to find your passion and practice it; but to share with you that when it seems you have diverged and you are struggling in a role that makes you less than happy, never fear — your path could be very near.

So, here are some additional considerations:

1. Write down what you like most about your job. Then write down other duties or jobs that you would like to do.

2. Write down what you most like to do in your personal life. Now combine this list with the list from #1 above to create the draft job description for your perfect job.

3. Now look for opportunities within your current company to do more of the tasks you enjoy, formally (job transfer or promotion) or informally (job shadowing, mentoring). If there are none, consider volunteer work or other opportunities that will give you some exposure to those tasks. You may find that you do not love what you thought you would. It is better to find that out in a volunteer role than a paying job. Continue to expand your circle until you find the opportunities you seek.

4. Network, network, network! Find a business partner or colleague who can help you find the path to get where you want to be

(Chamber of Commerce, professional or trade associations, former instructors, current or former bosses, colleagues).

5. Pay it forward! Once you get where you want to be, thank those who helped get you there, then find someone who is not there yet and serve as his mentor.

6. Now go practice your passion and enjoy your success and happiness!

Appendix A

PRE-TERMINATION CHECKLIST

Item	Description	Yes	No
1. Forewarning	Do you have documentation that shows what, how and when you informed the employee of the expectations this is not currently met?		
2. Evidence	Do you have evidence to back up your position such as: (1) the employee's own admission; (2) witnesses; or (3) tangible evidence?		
3. Proper Investigation	Prior to making your final decision, have you gotten the employee's side of the story and interviewed potential witnesses?		
4. Lack of Discrimination	Have you treated other employees who have been similarly situated the same? If not, is there a reason for treating this employee differently, which is job related and consistent with business necessity?		
5. Penalty Meets the Offense	Is it reasonable to think there is any action you could take, other than termination, that would correct the employee's behavior e.g., have you documented previous coaching, counseling and corrective action?		
6. Policy versus Practice	Is termination consistent with your policy and your past practice? If not, see # 4 above.		
7. Demographics	Does this termination follow any particular trend in the same department, business unit or across your organization related to protected status such as age, race, or gender? If yes, do you know why?		
8. Recent Events	Has this employee recently engaged in any protected activity such as expressing concerns about wages, hours, or conditions of employment or had any occurrence outside the usual course of business such as filing a workers' compensation claim, seeking FMLA leave, informing you of a medical condition such as pregnancy, etc?		

Endnotes

Chapter 1

[1] [(# days absent in month) ÷ (average # of employees during mo.) x (# of workdays)] x 100. See SHRM's "HR Metrics Toolkit." Available at www.shrm.org/hrdisciplines/Pages/CMS_005910.aspx.

[2] MONT CODE ANN § 39-2-904.

[3] The Society for Human Resource Management (SHRM), for example, offers its members a variety of toolkits that include spreadsheets and formulas for tracking this data. See SHRM's "Toolkits." Available at www.shrm.org/TemplatesTools/Toolkits /Pages/default.aspx.

[4] See "Understanding Waivers of Discrimination Claims in Employee Severance Agreements," The U.S. Equal Employment Opportunity Commission. Available at www.eeoc.gov/policy/docs/qanda _severance-agreements.html.

[5] Ibid.

Chapter 2

[1] Cali Ressler and Jody Thompson, "Make Results Matter," SHRM, July 1, 2009. Available at www.shrm.org/TemplatesTools/Samples /SupervisoryNewsletter/Pages/MakeResultsMatter.aspx.

[2] "Why Performance Management Improves Human Capital ROI," SHRM, June 1, 2007, citing Kotter, J., & Heskett, J. (1992). *Corporate culture and performance.* New York: The Free Press.

[3] See www.shrm.org/hrdisciplines/compensation/Pages/perfpay.aspx.

[4] SHRM®/ PDI 2000 Performance Management Survey, p. 6.

[5] SHRM®/ PDI 2000 Performance Management Survey, p. 10.

[6] "Managing Employee Performance," SHRM, June 15, 2009. Available at www.shrm.org/Research/Articles/Articles/Pages /ManagingEmployeePerformance.aspx.

[7] Laurence J. Peter and Raymond Hill, *The Peter Principle: Why Things Always Go Wrong* (New York: Morrow, 1969). Also see "Peter Principle." Available at http://en.wikipedia.org/wiki /Peter_Principle.

Chapter 3

[1] See http://thinkexist.com/quotes/theodore_isaac_rubin/.

[2] See www.acronymfinder.com.

[3] See "Learning Theories/Adult Learning." Available at http://en .wikibooks.org/wiki/Learning_TheoriesAdult_Learning _Theories.

[4] See "Pareto principle" at www.ask.com/wiki/Pareto_principle.

[5] See "Josh Billings" at http://en.wikipedia.org/wiki/Josh_Billings.

[6] *Connick v. Myers*, 461 U.S. 138 (1983).

Chapter 4

[1] "The Americans with Disabilities Act Amendments Act of 2008," U.S. Equal Employment Opportunity Commission. Available at www.eeoc.gov/laws/statutes/adaaa_info.cfm.

[2] "Notice Concerning The Americans With Disabilities Act (ADA) Amendments Act of 2008," U.S. Equal Employment Opportunity Commission. Available at www.eeoc.gov/ada/amendments _notice.html.

[3] See "Definitions," 29 CFR 1630.2. Available at http://edocket.access
.gpo.gov/cfr_2001/julqtr/pdf/29cfr1630.2.pdf.

[4] See "Covered Employer," U.S. Department of Labor. Available at
www.dol.gov/dol/allcfr/ESA/Title_29/Part_825/29CFR825
.104.htm.

[5] See "Eligible Employee," U.S. Department of Labor. Available at
www.dol.gov/dol/allcfr/ESA/Title_29/Part_825/29CFR825
.110.htm.

[6] See "Qualifying reasons for leave, general rule," U.S. Department of
Labor. Available at www.dol.gov/dol/allcfr/ESA/Title_29
/Part_825/29CFR825.112.htm.

[7] See "Leave to care for a covered servicemember with a serious injury
or illness," U.S. Department of Labor. Available at www.dol.gov
/dol/allcfr/ESA/Title_29/Part_825/29CFR825.127.htm.

[8] See "Employer notice requirements," U.S. Department of Labor.
Available at www.dol.gov/dol/allcfr/ESA/Title_29/Part_825
/29CFR825.300.htm.

[9] See "Notice of Eligibility and Rights & Responsibilities (Family and
Medical Leave Act)," U.S. Department of Labor, Employment
Standards Administration, Wage and Hour Division. Available
at www.dol.gov/whd/forms/WH-381.pdf.

[10] See "Designation Notice (Family and Medical Leave Act)," U.S.
Department of Labor, Employment Standards Administration,
Wage and Hour Division. Available at www.dol.gov/whd/forms
/WH-382.pdf.

[11] See "Employee notice requirements for foreseeable FMLA leave,"
U.S. Department of Labor. Available at www.dol.gov/dol/allcfr
/ESA/Title_29/Part_825/29CFR825.302.htm.

[12] See "Employee notice requirements for unforeseeable FMLA leave,"
U.S. Department of Labor. Available at www.dol.gov/dol/allcfr
/ESA/Title_29/Part_825/29CFR825.303.htm.

[13] See "Protection for employees who request leave or otherwise assert
FMLA rights," U.S. Department of Labor. Available at www.
dol.gov/dol/allcfr/ESA/Title_29/Part_825/29CFR825.220.htm.

[14] See "Serious Health Condition," U.S. Department of Labor. Available at www.dol.gov/dol/allcfr/ESA/Title_29/Part_825/29CFR825.113.htm.

[15] See "Protection for employees who request leave or otherwise assert FMLA rights," U.S. Department of Labor. Available at www.dol.gov/dol/allcfr/ESA/Title_29/Part_825/29CFR825.220.htm.

[16] See "Equivalent position," U.S. Department of Labor. Available at www.dol.gov/dol/allcfr/ESA/Title_29/Part_825/29CFR825.215.htm.

[17] See "Authentication and clarification of medical certification for leave taken because of an employee's own serious health condition or the serious health condition of a family member; second and third opinions," U.S. Department of Labor. Available at www.dol.gov/dol/allcfr/ESA/Title_29/Part_825/29CFR825.307.htm.

[18] "Uniformed Services Employment and Reemployment Rights Act (USERRA) Information," U.S. Department of Labor. Available at www.dol.gov/vets/programs/userra/main.htm.

[19] See "State Voting Leave Laws," SHRM. Available at www.shrm.org/LegalIssues/StateandLocalResources/StateandLocalStatutes andRegulations/Documents/statevotinglaw.pdf.

[20] See "Amount of Leave," U.S. Department of Labor, 29 CFR 825.200(e). Available at www.dol.gov/dol/allcfr/title_29/Part_825/29CFR825.200.htm.

Chapter 5

[1] See "Johari window" at http://en.wikipedia.org/wiki/Johari_window.

[2] "Results of the WBI U.S. Workplace Bullying Survey," Workplace Bullying Institute. Available at www.workplacebullying.org/research/WBI-Zogby2007Survey.html. Also see Teresa A. Daniel, *Stop Bullying at Work: Strategies and Tools for HR and Legal Professionals* (Alexandria, VA: SHRM, 2009).

[3] "Results of the 2010 WBI U.S. Workplace Bullying Survey," Workplace Bullying Institute. Available at www.workplacebullying.org/research/WBI-NatlSurvey2010.html.

Chapter 6

[1] The states are Colorado, Connecticut, Illinois, Indiana, Kentucky, Louisiana, Maryland, Massachusetts, Michigan, Minnesota, Nebraska, New Hampshire, New Jersey, New Mexico, New York, Oregon, Rhode Island, Utah, Vermont, and Washington.

[2] See "Independent Contractor or Employee," Department of Treasury, Internal Revenue Service, Publication 1779 (Rev. 8-2008). Available at www.irs.gov/pub/irs-pdf/p1779.pdf.

[3] See "Fact Sheet #71: Internship Programs Under the Fair Labor Standards Act," U.S. Department of Labor, Wage and Hour Division (April 2010). Available at www.dol.gov/whd/regs /compliance/whdfs71.pdf.

[4] "Montana Code Annotated 2009," Montana Legislative Services. Available at http://data.opi.mt.gov/bills/mca/39/2/39-2-904.htm

[5] "FairPay," Department of Labor, Wage and Hour Division. Available at www.dol.gov/whd/regs/compliance/fairpay/.

[6] See "Amount of salary required," U.S. Department of Labor, 29 CFR 541.600. Available at www.dol.gov/dol/allcfr/title_29/ Part_541/29CFR541.600.htm.

[7] See "Salary basis," U.S. Department of Labor, 29 CFR 541.602. Available at www.dol.gov/dol/allcfr/title_29/Part_541 /29CFR541.602.htm.

[8] See "FLSA2005-46," U.S. Department of Labor. Available at www .dol.gov/whd/opinion/FLSA/2005/2005_10_28_46_FLSA .htm and http://www.dol.gov/whd/opinion/FLSA/2005/2005 _10_24_41_FLSA.htm.

[9] See www.dol.gov/whd/opinion/FLSA/2006/2006_03_10_07_FLSA .pdf.

[10] See "2008 Statistics Fact Sheet," U.S. Department of Labor, Wage and Hour Division. Available at www.dol.gov/whd/statistics /2008FiscalYear.htm.

[11] See "General rule for executive employees," U.S. Department of Labor, 29 CFR 541.100. Available at www.dol.gov/dol/allcfr/title _29/part_541/29CFR541.100.htm.

[12] See "General rule for administrative employees," U.S. Department of Labor, 29 CFR 541.200. Available at www.dol.gov/dol/allcfr/ title_29/Part_541/29CFR541.200.htm.

[13] The states are Alabama, Arkansas, California, Colorado, Connecticut, Hawaii, Illinois, Kentucky, Minnesota, Missouri, New Jersey, North Dakota, Oregon, Pennsylvania, Washington, West Virginia, and Wisconsin.

Chapter 7

[1] "Enforcement Guidance on Vicarious Employer Liability for Unlawful Harassment by Supervisors," U.S. Equal Employment Opportunity Commission. Available at www.eeoc.gov/policy/docs/ harassment.html.

[2] See "Effect of improper deductions from salary," U.S. Department of Labor, 29 CFR 541.603(d). Available at www.dol.gov/DOL/ allcfr/esa/Title_29/Part_541/29CFR541.603.htm.

[3] "Model Salary Basis Policy: Overtime Security for the 21st Century Workforce," U.S. Department of Labor. Available at www.dol .gov/whd/regs/compliance/fairpay/modelPolicy_PF.htm.

[4] *Cloutier v. Costco Wholesale Corp.*, 390 F.3d 126 (1st Cir. 2004).

[5] *EEOC v. Red Robin Gourmet Burgers, Inc.*, 2005 WL 2090677 (W.D. Wash. Aug. 29, 2005).

[6] See "Section 12: Religious Discrimination," EEOC Compliance Manual, U.S. Equal Employment Opportunity Commission. Available at www.eeoc.gov/policy/docs/religion.html.

[7] See "Questions and Answers About Employer Responsibilities Concerning the Employment of Muslims, Arabs, South Asians, and Sikhs," U.S. Equal Employment Opportunity Commission. Available at www.eeoc.gov/facts/backlash-employer.html. See also "Questions and Answers: Religious Discrimination in the Workplace," U.S. Equal Employment Opportunity Commission. Available at www.eeoc.gov/policy/docs/qanda_religion.html.

Chapter 8

[1] "Employee Engagement: A Leading Indicator of Financial Performance," Gallup (n.d.). Available at www.gallup.com/consulting/52/Employee-Engagement.aspx.

Foreword

[1] "Despite Grumbling, Most Americans Say They Are Happy At Work," *ScienceDaily* (August 28, 2007). Available at www.sciencedaily.com/releases/2007/08/070827124647.htm.

[2] "Over Half of Americans Say They Are 'Very Happy' at Work, According to SnagAJob.com Survey," *Newshound* (August 28, 2007). Available at www.associatedcontent.com/article/360505/over_half_of_americans_say_they_are.html.

Index

80-20 rule *See* Pareto Principle

A

absenteeism, 2, 7, 40, 91
adult learning theory, 45
adverse employment action, 19, 20,
    71, 90
adverse impact, 9, 17
affirmative action, 9, 88
Age Discrimination in Employment Act
    (ADEA), 10, 14
Americans with Disabilities Act (ADA),
    6, 53, 57, 58, 59, 60, 61, 72, 74, 103
Americans with Disabilities Act Amend-
    ments Act (ADAAA), 57
assault and battery, 80, 81
attendance, 7, 22, 23, 27, 28, 30, 32,
    34, 40, 68, 94, 112, 119
at-will, 8, 39, 70, 85, 90, 91, 99, 102,
    104

B

behavior(s), 1, 4, 7, 8, 20, 21, 22, 26, 27,
    29, 30, 31, 33, 34, 43, 46, 53, 54,
    78, 80, 81, 83, 127
behaviorally anchored rating systems
    (BARS), 30
Billings, Josh, 51
bullying, 80, 83

C

career ladders, 122
coaching, 16, 21, 22, 24, 39, 40, 55, 81,
    101, 127
collective bargaining agreement(s)
    (CBA), 8, 91
competency/ies, 30, 33
compliance audit, 74, 84
conflict, 19, 33, 34, 35
correcting, 24, 39, 40, 46, 50, 55, 101
corrective action, 5, 6, 7, 8, 9, 16, 19,
    20, 21, 22, 46, 47, 48, 49, 54, 55, 71,
    90, 104, 113, 116, 127
cost of living adjustments (COLA), 35,
    47
counseling, 16, 21, 22, 24, 39, 40, 43,
    50, 55, 64, 101, 127
credibility assessment, 4

D

defamation, 80, 81
demographics, 9, 10, 127
demotion, 90
Department of Labor, U.S. (DOL), 66,
    68, 69, 72, 89, 92, 95, 96, 106
discharge(s), 9, 70, 90
disciplinary action *See* corrective action
discrimination, 6, 10, 12, 13, 32, 39, 59,
    72, 73, 79, 103, 109, 110, 127

E
EEO-1, 9
emotional distress, 50, 80, 81
employee assistance program (EAP),
    53, 54, 112
employee handbook, 8, 9, 14, 17, 46,
    47, 74, 84, 101-13
employment practices liability insurance
    (EPLI), 73, 74, 84
engagement, 117
equal employment opportunity (EEO),
    73, 102-4
Equal Employment Opportunity Com-
    mission, U.S. (EEOC), vii, 10, 12, 57,
    58, 59, 103, 109, 110
ERISA, 87
Error of Central Tendency, 28, 34
escalator clause, 70
essential functions, 27, 59
exit interviews, 10, 11, 12

F
Fair Labor Standards Act (FLSA), 88,
    90, 91, 99, 106
false imprisonment, 50, 80, 81
Family and Medical Leave Act (FMLA),
    10, 47, 48, 55, 61-8, 70-3, 87, 95,
    102, 107, 112, 127

G
The Gallup Organization, 117
graphic rating scales, 30-1

H
Halo Effect, 33
harassment, 13, 73, 75, 77, 78, 79, 80,
    81, 83, 84, 94, 102, 103, 104, 112
Health Insurance Portability and Ac-
    countability Act (HIPAA), 68, 82
Healthy Families Act, 71
Hull, Raymond, 33

I
independent contractor(s) (IC), 85-7, 99
Ingham, Harry, 76
intern(s), 85, 87-9, 99, 123
Internal Revenue Service (IRS), 86, 87
introductory period, 32, 35, 104, 105,
    112

J
job classification(s), 11, 15, 22, 98, 120
job shadowing, 24, 89, 119-20, 125
Johari Window, 75, 76
just cause, 91

K
knowledge, skills, and abilities (KSA),
    30, 41, 42, 44

L
leave, 8, 9, 10, 23, 57-74, 87, 93, 95,
    101, 105, 106, 107-08, 112
    jury, 71, 94, 112
    military, 55, 63, 69-70, 94, 112
    parental, 71-2
    voting, 71, 74
    witness, 71, 94
legally protected class(es), 6, 78, 80,
    84, 90
Leniency Error, 35
Luft, Joseph, 76

M
management by objectives (MBO), 31
mentoring, 24, 125

N
new employee orientation (NEO), 2, 32,
    36, 40, 115, 116, 118, 119, 120

O
Older Workers Benefit Protection Act
    (OWBPA), 13
onboarding, 36, 115, 117, 119, 120, 121,
    122
on-the-job-training (OJT), 120
open-ended questions, 54

P
Pareto Principle, 46
pay-for-performance, 35, 68
performance, 2, 4, 5, 8, 19, 20, 22, 24,
    25, 26, 27, 28, 30, 31, 33, 34, 35, 36,
    46, 48, 50, 53, 81, 106, 120

appraisal(s), 19, 20, 21, 22, 24,
    25, 26, 27, 28, 29, 30, 32, 33,
    34, 35, 36, 48, 49, 101, 112,
    119
    deficiencies, 50
    development, 24, 26
    effectiveness, 25
        errors, 78
    evaluation(s), 24, 29, 35
    issues, 53
    management, 24
    plans, 26
    poor performance, 9, 34, 91
    problems, 16, 45
    record, 48
    review, 24
    standards, 2, 43
performance-enhancing cultures, 25
The Peter Principle, 33
Peter, Laurence J., 33
pre-employment assessments, 115
Primacy Effect, 33-4
privacy, 49, 68, 80, 82

R
Rubin, Theodore, 39

S
severance, 13-5, 66
similarly situated, 7, 48, 78, 127
Society for Human Resource Manage-
    ment (SHRM), 25, 72, 74, 85
stay interviews, 11, 121

T
tardiness, 2, 57
Title VII of the Civil Rights Act of 1964,
    72, 79, 80, 103, 108
training, 4, 8, 12, 24, 31, 35, 37, 75, 78,
    81, 84, 86, 88, 101, 121
turnover, 11, 121

U
unemployment insurance (UI), 1, 15-6,
    49, 86, 108
Uniform Services Employment and Re-
    employment Rights Act (USERRA),
    69, 70
union, 32, 87, 91, 116

V
volunteer(s), 85, 87-90, 99, 125

W
workers' compensation, 10, 55, 86, 87,
    94, 113, 127
Workplace Bullying Institute (WBI), 83

Z
Zogby International, 83

Acknowledgements

To Mark — my husband, who did not bat an eye in 2002 and promptly responded, "Go for it!" when I asked what he thought about my starting my own practice. Thank you for your constant and unwavering confidence, support, and love. I absolutely could not have done this without you.

To Mom and Dad — you laid the foundation that made this book (and any success I might humbly say I have) possible. Thank you for teaching me the value of a strong work ethic, kindness, and honor.

To Janet — you have been, are, and will continue to be my mentor and friend for life. You trusted me and gave me the opportunities to learn, grow, and succeed. Thank you for your confidence, trust, support, and friendship.

To Vicki — my friend and colleague who let me ride on your coattails from time to time, selflessly sharing your tips for success and pitfalls to avoid. Thank you for sharing and for your friendship.

About the Author

Christine V. Walters, MAS, J.D., SPHR, has nearly 25 years of combined experience in HR administration, management, employment law practice, and teaching. She has been engaged as an expert witness, and testified before the U.S. Congress, state legislative committees, and federal administrative agencies. Ms. Walters has been interviewed and quoted in a variety of media, including television, radio, and print media.

Throughout her career, Ms. Walters has been honored with awards and accolades, including:

- Small Business of the Year Award — Carroll County Chamber of Commerce, November 2010

- Small Business of the Year Award — B/W Corridor Chamber of Commerce, April 2010

- Nominee — Daily Record's "Leadership in Law" Award, 2009

- Finalist — Maryland Chamber of Commerce Small Business of the Year Award, 2009

- President's Award — B/W Corridor Chamber of Commerce, 2003

- Capitol Award — Society for Human Resource Management (SHRM), 2002

- Outstanding Leadership Award — American Society for Healthcare Human Resource Administration (ASHHRA), 1997

- Best Practices Award — ASHHRA, 1996

Ms. Walters has presented at national, regional, and state conferences across the country, including the Society for Human Resource Management (SHRM), Employment Management Association (EMA), the American Physical Therapy Association, College and University Personnel Association, Credit Union National Association, and more.

Today, Ms. Walters serves as an independent consultant doing business as FiveL Company, *Helping Leaders Limit Their Liability by Learning the Law*[SM], providing proactive guidance, training programs, education, and counsel on employment and HR issues, policies, procedures, and practices for clients across the country and in a variety of industries. She was also an adjunct faculty member of the Johns Hopkins University, teaching a variety of courses in the graduate, undergraduate, and certification level programs from 1999 through 2006.

Ms. Walters demonstrates her commitment to supporting and advancing the needs and interests of the business community and HR profession by serving in a variety of volunteer leadership roles, including and not limited to:

- Secretary — Maryland SHRM State Council
- Executive and HR Committees — Carroll County Chamber of Commerce
- President, Carroll County SHRM
- Editorial Advisory Board Member — Thompson Publishing's FMLA Handbook
- Board Member — Maryland Chamber of Commerce
- Board Member — Hunt Valley Business Forum
- Advisory Board Member — McDaniel College, Graduate Program in Human Resources
- Former Member — SHRM's Legislative Action and Employee Relations Committees

Ms. Walters is licensed to practice law in the state of Maryland.